Saints and heroes since the Middle Ages — George Hodges

Publisher's Note

The book descriptions we ask booksellers to display prominently warn that this is an historic book with numerous typos or missing text; it is not indexed or illustrated.

The book was created using optical character recognition software. The software is 99 percent accurate if the book is in good condition. However, we do understand that even one percent can be an annoying number of typos! And sometimes all or part of a page may be missing from our copy of the book. Or the paper may be so discolored from age that it is difficult to read. We apologize and gratefully acknowledge Google's assistance.

After we re-typeset and design a book, the page numbers change so the old index and table of contents no longer work. Therefore, we often remove them; otherwise, please ignore them.

We carefully proof read any book that will sell enough copies to pay the proof reader; unfortunately, most don't. So instead we try to let customers download a free copy of the original typo-free book. Simply enter the barcode number from the back cover of the paperback in the Free Book form at www.RareBooksClub.com. You may also qualify for a free trial membership in our book club to download up to four books for free. Simply enter the barcode number from the back cover onto the membership form on our home page. The book club entitles you to select from more than a million books at no additional charge. Simply enter the title or subject onto the search form to find the books.

If you have any questions, could you please be so kind as to consult our Frequently Asked Questions page at www.RareBooksClub.com/faqs.cfm? You are also welcome to contact us there.

General Books LLC™, Memphis, USA, 2012.

∗ ∗ ∗ ∗ ∗ ∗ ∗ ∗

Since the Middle Ages
BY
GEORGE HODGES
Author of
"Saints and Heroes to the End of the Middle Ages," etc.
WITH ILLUSTRATIONS
Copyright, 1912,
Y
HENRY HOLT AND COMPANY
Published October, 191a
THE QUINN BODEN CO. PRESS
RAH WAY, N. J.
CONTENTS
PAGE
Luther, 1483-1546.... 3
More, 1478-1535 29
Loyola, 1491-1556 53
Cranmer, 1489-1556.... 74
Calvin, 1509-1564.... 98
Knox, 1505-1572 122
g COLIGNY, 1519-1572...-145
William The Silent, 1533-1584. 168
Brewster, 1560-1644.... 191
Laud, i573-!645 211
$ Cromwell, 1599-165 8.... 233
V J BUNYAN, 1628-1688. -257
J Fox, 1624-1691 277
Wesley, 1703-1791.... 296
S
«,,o$
ILLUSTRATIONS
The Embarkation Of The
Martin Luther
Sir Thomas More
St. Ignatius Loyola.
Thomas Cranmer
John Calvin
John Knox...
Gaspard De Coligny.
William The Silent.
William Laud
Oliver Cromwell
John Bunyan
George Fox.
John Wesley
Pilgrims *Frontispiece* PAGE 3 29 53 74 .. 98 122 145. 168 211 233 257 277.

---

296 SAINTS AND HEROES SINCE THE MIDDLE AGES MARTIN LUTHER

From a Print in the Possession of the New York Public Library LUTHER 1483-1546

On the last day of October, in the year 1517, a German monk posted a paper on a church door in Wittenberg. It was written in Latin, and was addressed to theologians. It contained a series of statements concerning the doctrine and practice of indulgences. The writer desired to have the matter discussed. It seemed to him that there was something wrong about it, and he would be glad to hear what wiser men might say. Here, he said, are indulgences preached and sold throughout the Church: is it right? is it in accordance with the gospel and the truth? The paper was a question.

Now the meaning of an indulgence was this. Every sin deserves the punishment of God. The sure consequence of 3 sin is eternal suffering in hell. But by the grace of God, and the cross of Christ, and the ministry of the Church, there is a way of escape. Every sin may be forgiven, if the sinner is truly sorry and repents. In order, however, to obtain this forgiveness, the repentant sinner, they said, must confess his sin to a priest, and be, by him, assured of the pardon of God, and in addition must do what the priest tells him as a penance. The priest, in the old time, told him to fast, or to give money to the poor, or to go on a pilgrimage. In the days of the crusades, sinners were told that, in the place of the former penances, they might enlist as soldiers in the armies which were going to the Holy Land to take Jerusalem from the Turks. By-and-by, they were told that they might be assured of forgiveness if they paid the expenses of somebody else who was willing to go in their place. Then they were told they might gain the same blessing by giving money for some other good purpose; for example, for the building of a church. These substitutes for the old penances were called indulgences.

Gradually and naturally, this doctrine gave rise to grave errors and evils. One of the errors was that simple and ignorant people easily believed that the forgiveness of God was gained, not by repentance, but by indulgence. If they sinned, they could make it right, they thought, and escape punishment, by the payment of money. And this payment, they imagined, would affect them, not only in this world, but in the world to come; and would obtain pardon not only for themselves, but for others who had gone already into that other world. One of the evils was that this error was made a means of raising money for the Church. People gladly paid for the building of cathedrals and monasteries in the belief that they were thereby gaining forgiveness for their sins, and salvation for their souls and for the souls of their friends.

So when Pope Leo X wished to raise a great sum of money for the rebuilding of St. Peter's Church at Rome, he undertook to do it by the sale of indulgences. It seemed as right in those days to build a church by means of indulgences as it seemed right in this country a hundred years ago to build a church by means of lotteries. The raising of this money in Germany was put into the hands of a man named Tetzel. He was a frank, straightforward person, with a better head for business than for religion, but with a great ability to appeal to the people. He knew how to speak to crowds. Tetzel took the doctrine of indulgences as he found it, and used it, as the phrase is, for all it was worth. He went about as a revival preacher goes to-day, having preparations made for his coming, enlisting all the ministers of the place, and holding great meetings. But his purpose was simply to get money. He began by preaching about sin and about hell. Now, he said, what have you done? All sins may be forgiven. Here is the promise of the pope, here are letters of indulgence, here is the opportunity for a little money to save your souls. And your friends,— perhaps you have a father or a mother, perhaps you have children, gone into the other world, in purgatory,—you may save them also. "Do you not hear your dead parents crying out, ' Have mercy upon us? We are in sore pain and you can set us free for a mere pittance? '"

This was what Martin Luther had in mind when he posted his paper concerning indulgences on the church door in Wittenberg.

Luther was already one of the foremost men in the Church in Germany. Born the son of a miner, among hills filled with copper, he had made his way by his own efforts through school and college, and had begun to study law. Suddenly, amidst the terrors of a thunderstorm, he had changed his mind and had given himself to the ministry. He had entered a monastery in Erfurt. There he had gone through long seasons of deep depression, trying to save his soul by fasting and pain and prayer. For days he went without food, for nights he went without sleep, hoping thus to gain the good-will of God. He was terribly afraid of God, and feared that he would be lost at last in the torments of hell. But in the monastery he found wise advisers. One good brother said, "Martin, you are a fool. God is not angry with you; it is you who are angry with God. " Another good brother, Staupitz, the head of the monastery, to whom Luther cried, "Oh, my sin, my sin, my sin!" replied, "You have no real sin. You make a sin out of every trifle." Staupitz urged him to trust in the mercy and love of God who freely forgives those who put their faith in Christ. He saw also that what Luther needed was an active life, and to be occupied, not in thinking about himself, but in ministering to others.

Then Staupitz became dean of the theological faculty of the University of Wittenberg, and he called Luther out of the monastery to be professor of logic and ethics. Presently he sent him on an errand to Rome, to see a bit of the great world. On his return Luther took his degree of doctor of divinity, and began to preach in the city church. He was appointed to teach theology to the young monks in the Wittenberg monastery, and men came to be instructed by him till the place was overcrowded. When he was but thirty-one he was made district-vicar, and put in charge of eleven monasteries. His hands were full of business. Then Staupitz made him his successor, in the chair of biblical theology.

There was already a new interest in the study of the Bible, and Luther entered into his new duties with enthusiasm, learning Greek and Hebrew, and reading all the latest books. He was at the same time the most popular preacher in the town, and the most popular professor in the university; and his fame began to go abroad. He had a practical mind, and was interested, not only in doctrine, but in conduct. And he had a remarkably strong and free and original way of expressing himself. Thus he criticised the common way of thinking about the saints. Instead of trying to be like them, people were praying to the saints to help them. "We honor them," said Luther, "and call upon them only when we have a pain in our legs or our head, or when our pockets are empty."

This was the man who posted on his church door a proposition that the theologians should look seriously into the matter of indulgences.

Luther's thesis, as his paper was called, set all Europe talking. People were ready for great changes. It was as when the spring comes after a long winter, and the brooks begin to flow again, and the grass grows green, and buds appear upon the trees. The invention of the mariner's compass had enabled Columbus to steer due west across the Atlantic, and the new land which he had discovered showed that the world was much bigger than men had thought. The invention of powder and of printing had given men a gun in one hand and a book in the other, which were changing the conditions of society. The plain man with the gun was able to face the knight on horseback, and the plain man with the book was able to test the teachings of the scholar. It was the day of a new independence.

Thus, although Luther's questions as to the doctrine of indulgences were received by the theologians with suspicion and by the authorities with alarm, in both Church and state, the common people heard them gladly. They were translated out of Latin into German. "In fourteen days," says Luther, "the theses ran through all Germany; for the whole world was complaining of indulgences." And of other matters also; of other evils in religion, against which there seemed to have at last appeared a leader.

For the indulgences had been sold in the name of the pope, and by his authority; and Tetzel, in defending them, had declared that the pope could do no wrong. "The pope," said Tetzel, "cannot err in those things which are of faith and necessary to salvation." And to this he added, "They who speak slightingly of the honor and authority of the pope are guilty of blasphemy."

And the pope was against Luther. At first, he had considered the theses as of no importance. "A drunken German wrote them," he is reported to have said. "When he is sober, he will think differently." But the more he heard about the matter, the less he liked it. Then he summoned Luther to Rome to be put on trial. And Luther, being protected by his prince, the Elector Frederick, refused to go.

Miltitz, on behalf of the pope, met him with persuasions to hold his peace. He told him that if he would change his mind the pope would make him a bishop, or an archbishop, or a cardinal. Eck, on behalf of the pope, met him with arguments. He told him that his opinions were like those for which John Hus had been burned at the stake.

Luther, on his side, appealed, at first, from the pope ill-informed to the pope better-informed, and then from the pope to a general council of the Church. The question of indulgences fell into the background. The debate now turned upon the power of the pope. Was he indeed the representative of Christ on earth, in such a sense that his word was truth, and his will was law? Luther declared his determination to think for himself, and to make up his own mind, and to say that which he believed to be right and true. He would be bound, he said, neither by the pope nor by the Church. He would be guided by the Bible and his own conscience.

There are two ancient and universal parties in religion. On one side are those who are interested in the institution, in services and sacraments, in customs and traditions. They were represented in the Old Testament by the priests, in the New Testament by the Scribes and Pharisees. On the other side are those who are interested in the individual, in the relation of religion to actual, present conditions. They were represented in the Old Testament by the prophets, in the New Testament by the apostles. The motto of one party is "It is written"; they refer to law and authority, and desire to keep in the old ways. The motto of the other party is "It seems good to the Holy Ghost and to us"; they refer to the voice of God speaking in their own souls, and are ready to change as their knowledge of the truth changes, or their understanding of the needs of men. One party is conservative, the other is progressive. They are both right, but they are never both right at the same time. Now the conservatives are right, and contend on the side of God against the progressives who are attacking that which is both old and true, and are throwing the Church into disorder. Now the progressives are right, and contend on the side of God against the conservatives who are maintaining that which is not only old but mistaken, and are trying to keep out the light, and are resisting reformation.

In Luther's time it was the progressives who were right, and he was the leader of them.

Matters came rapidly to a crisis. In 1520, the pope issued a bull of excommunication against Luther. The word bull is from the Latin *bulla,* meaning the leaden seal which was attached to important documents. It came to be applied to the documents themselves. The effect of an excommunication was to expel the offender, not only from the Holy Communion, but from intercourse with his neighbors; nobody was allowed to trade with him or speak to him. This, however, depended on public opinion. In order to make an excommunication effective, people must believe that the pope had the power to issue it, and that in issuing it he was expressing the will of

God. Wherever this was not believed, the bull was worth no more than the paper on which it was written. Already there were so many persons in Germany who were disposed to disregard the pope, that Luther, when he received the bull, called together the professors and students of the university and burned the thing.

And so strongly was Luther supported by the nobles, the lawyers, the priests, and the people of Germany, that in spite of the excommunication he was permitted to plead his cause before the emperor, and the representatives of the states and cities of the land. The council met at Worms, and to that city Luther went in spite of dangers. He knew that he might be set upon by the way and killed: he knew that he might be condemned and burned alive, as Hus had been. He said afterwards, "Had I known as many devils would set upon me as there were tiles on the roofs, I should have sprung into the midst of them with joy."

Thus he stood before the representatives and rulers of Church and state. A pile of books which he had published was upon the table. They asked him if he wrote them, and he said that they were his. They asked him if he was prepared to stand by all that he had written, and he answered that some of the books were composed of sermons, concerning which nobody had raised a question: some were controversies with various persons, whom he had, perhaps, called harder names than was necessary, for he did not claim to be a saint; some were against the pope; he was prepared to stand by these, and to withdraw from them not a word. Nevertheless, he was willing to change his mind, if he could be proved wrong out of the Bible. "You demand a simple reply," he said, "and I will give it. Unless convinced by the testimony of Scripture or by clear reason, I cannot and will not revoke anything, for it is neither safe nor right to act against one's conscience. God help me. Amen."

The result was a formal condemnation. Luther's books were to be burned, nobody was to be allowed to read them, he himself was to be seized and sent to the emperor to be put in prison. Thus he was under the ban of the state as well as of the Church, and was declared an outlaw. This decision continued without repeal all the rest of Luther's life. But it had no more effect than the pope's bull. For even the laws of the civil courts depend on the will of the people. Luther lived all his days thereafter under the protection of the people.

For the moment, however, it seemed prudent to remove him from the hands of his enemies. One night, as he was taking his journey, returning from Worms to Wittenberg, he was met in a lonely road by a company of armed horsemen, his companions were put to flight, and he was taken by secret paths through the woods to the castle of the Wartburg. There he found himself among friends, who had taken this way to bring him into a safe hiding-place. He lived in this friendly imprisonment for nearly a year, while all the world wondered what had become of him. That he was still alive was made plain by the fact that he continued to write and publish letters, tracts, and pamphlets. One time the Archbishop of Mayence ventured to begin again the sale of indulgences, but on the receipt of a single letter from the hidden Luther he changed his plans in a fright.

It was during his year in the Wartburg that Luther made his translation of the New Testament out of Greek into German. Afterwards, with the help of others, he translated the Old Testament, completing the whole work in 1534. This became the Bible of the German people, and had the effect of determining the German language. It had been spoken in a great number of different dialects; thenceforth it was spoken and written in the manner of Luther. And thus appearing in a form which became the German of old Germany, the Bible was brought into the possession of all the people. The prophets and apostles spoke to them in their own speech.

Meanwhile, outside the Wartburg, and apart from the direction of Luther, events of importance were taking place. The Reformation was becoming a general movement. When Luther returned, he found much of which he disapproved. Rising up, as he did, in the face of authority, and declaring his individual and independent conviction, other men were moved to follow his example. And they were as ready to disagree with Luther as Luther had been ready to disagree with Rome. The Protestants were divided amongst themselves.

It was the desire of Luther to make few changes in religion. He felt that he and his followers were still in the ancient church, out of which, indeed, they had put the pope and the bishops and the superstition, but whose life and worship and ministry proceeded as before. But others, in the process of making changes, went on and on, till the difference between the old and the new became very great. They destroyed images and closed monasteries; they abandoned ancient customs, introduced strange services, and taught doctrines which had never been heard before.

Luther opposed, not only these radicals, but the great company of learned men called Humanists, who were led by Erasmus. They were quietly trying to establish truth on a basis of reason, and to encourage men to think freely, relying on the good sense and the good will of men. Luther, however, denied the freedom of the will, and put in the place of the authority of the Church the authority of the Bible. His idea was that men were not to reason about religion, but to take it just as they found it in the Scriptures. Thus he lost the support of the scholars.

At the same time the rebellion of Luther against the pope and the bishops was followed by men who rebelled against their employers and their masters. The Peasants' War was an uprising of the poor against the rich. They went about with clubs and torches, destroying property and lives. Luther's enemies declared that this was the natural consequence of Luther's teaching. He had cut the dikes of order and authority and obedience, they said, and, of course, the land was overflowed. Luther was as stout against the men who were claiming their right to live, as he was against those who were claiming their right to think. He denounced the peasants, and urged the princes to shoot them like mad dogs.

Thus he had his limitations, like most people, and having led the people a little way could conduct them no further. He did his great part, and others took up the work and continued it; as Columbus discovered America, but others settled it. Two things, however, Luther admirably taught. He taught the doctrine of salvation by faith, and the doctrine of the goodness of the common life.

When Luther came, men were being taught the doctrine of salvation by grace. Grace was a blessing given by God through the Church. It was bestowed by the priests in the sacraments. And that meant that the Church, the priests, and the sacraments were absolutely necessary to men in order to be saved. It made the Church a supreme power. Luther taught that salvation is by grace, but that grace is given to those who have faith. Faith is the act by which we perceive the love and forgiveness of God. It joins us to God; it gives the believer peace and joy and assurance of salvation. And it is independent of all means. It is between the individual and God, without the need of any priest. The love of God is revealed in the Bible, and it is set forth in the sacraments, but it is perceived by each person for himself. The effect of the doctrine was to set men free from the Church; they could get along without it, Luther said.

And this idea which made every man a priest to himself, and thus put away the distinction between the clergy and other people, made men see the goodness of all life. God is our father, and He made the world for us to enjoy. The Christian is not to turn his back upon it, and go out of it, but to enter into it freely and gladly, carrying on his business, having his family and friends, and behaving himself naturally. In a world where the ideal of a good life was a separation from all the common concerns and recreations of society, this was a new doctrine. "It looks like a great thing," said Luther, "when a monk renounces everything and goes into a cloister, carries on a life of asceticism, fasts, watches, prays, etc. On the other hand, it looks like a small thing when a maid cooks and cleans and does other housework. But because God's command is there, even such a small work must be praised as a service of God, far surpassing the holiness and asceticism of all monks and nuns. For here there is no command of God, but there God's command is fulfilled, that one should honor father and mother and help in the care of the home."

So Luther was married, and his wife, Katherine von Bora, made him a comfortable and happy home. Now he ate three good meals a day, and slept in a bed which was made up every morning, instead of once a year as when he lived alone. There he gathered his friends about him, and wrote his sermons and his books, and prepared the lectures which he gave in the University of Wittenberg. There he planted a garden, and dug a well; though Katherine could not persuade him to keep his study in order; books and papers were always in a pile upon his desk. He was busy unceasingly, directing a hundred enterprises, answering a hundred thousand questions, the counsellor of Protestants. He was often depressed to see how, after all, the Reformation had not very much reformed the world, and he had his share of pain and sickness.

Luther died in Eisleben, where he was born, and was buried in Wittenberg, where he lived most of his life. A greathearted man, frank, sincere, full of courage and strength, often angry, often merry, loving God and his friends, and hating evil, he had the qualities of a soldier and of a pioneer. He will always be remembered as the man who broke the power of the Mediaeval Church.

SIR THOMAS MORE
From the Painting after Holbein in the National Portrait Gallery MORE 1478-1535

A BOOK which Luther wrote on the "Babylonian Captivity of the Church" was answered in England by King Henry the Eighth. So stout was the orthodoxy of the king against the heresy of the reformer, that the pope conferred upon him the title, still borne by sovereigns of England, of Defender of the Faith. In this answer the king maintained that the pope was the greatest man in the world, and was to be obeyed, not only by all priests, but by all princes. He showed what he had written to Sir Thomas More, and More advised him not to publish it.

"You and the pope," he said, "may some time fall out, and disagree. Then you may find that you have put a sword in the pope's hand against yourself." To this excellent advice the king paid no attention.

Sir Thomas More was the most eminent man of his time in England. He was known all over Europe for his scholarship and his statesmanship. But the most interesting thing about him for us is the fact that he represented, better than anybody else, the mind of many wise and good men who were in sympathy with the new ideas which were at that time beginning to change the world, and yet in sympathy also with the old ways. He was the intimate friend of Erasmus, who was the leader of such men in Europe.

More and Erasmus saw clearly that the Church of their day ought to be reformed. They felt, for example, very much as Luther felt about indulgences. They knew that religion, among many people, had come to be a matter of magic, a belief that saints and relics could save them from the punishment of their sins, and from the diseases of their bodies, and could bring them good luck both in this world and in the next. And they knew that religion, among many priests, had come to be a matter of money; all that they cared for was to be rich. They desired to have these evils stopped. Thus they were in sympathy with the reforms which had been started by Luther. But, at the same time, they cared greatly for the Church. They saw that along with all that was wrong, there was much more that was right. And this they wished to keep. They feared that the Reformation would go too far. When they found that Luther, having attacked the indulgences, had proceeded to attack the pope who permitted them, and having defied the pope, had denied the necessity of the sacraments from which the pope had excommunicated him, they felt that he was like a man, who, finding a wasps' nest under the eaves of his house, burns out the nest with so great a fire that he burns the whole house with it.

Thus in a time when all the world was taking sides, some Protestant and others Catholic, some for the new and others for the old, More and Erasmus and such moderate men found themselves in a difficult position. They were on both sides, and on neither.

One time, while Henry the Seventh was the king, More, though he was but twentyfour years of age, was a member of Parliament; and the king demanded of the House of Commons a great sum of money, much more than he had any right to ask; and when the House was silent, being unwilling to vote the money, and yet unwilling to offend the king, More made a speech the effect of which was to give the king very much less than he had required. Some of the king's people told him that he had been defeated by a beardless boy. Coming thus under the ill-will of the king, he retired into private life. And there the debate between what was called the old learning and the new occupied his thoughts. At first, he studied Greek and science, like a man of the new time. Then he gave himself to devotion and prayer in a monastery, and planned to be a priest, like a man of the old time. The matter was happily decided for the moment by a visit which he made to Mr. Colt's house, in Essex, where he met his daughter Jane and married her. But it illustrates the contention in his mind between the new and the old.

Then the seventh Henry died, and the eighth Henry came to the throne, and More came out of his retirement into great favor. He was made a member of the Privy Council, and Treasurer of the Exchequer, and was chosen Speaker of

Parliament. The new king so delighted in his conversation that More could hardly get leave to go home from the court to his own family as much as once a month. The king would send for him to come to his private room, and there would talk with him sometimes about this world, sometimes about the next, and then would take him to the palace roof on clear nights, "there to consider with him the diversities, courses, motions, and operations of the stars and planets." And when More, tiring of this and desiring to go home, would stay away from court, the king would visit him in his own house, coming to dinner without being invited, and afterwards walking with More in the garden by the hour together with his arm about his neck.

William Roper, More's son-in-law, who wrote his life, congratulated him on this royal friendship. But More said, "Son Roper, I may tell thee I have no cause to be proud thereof; for if my head would win him a castle in France, it should not fail to go."

By-and-by, he was made Lord Chancellor; his father, in the meantime, being only a judge of the Court of the King's Bench. It is remembered that as Sir Thomas passed through Westminster Hall, he would often go into his father's court, and reverently kneel down and ask his father's blessing; and that when he and his father met in any place, "notwithstanding his high office, he would offer the pre-eminence to his father."

More became Lord Chancellor by reason of the fall of Cardinal Wolsey; and the fall of Cardinal Wolsey was occasioned by the difficulties connected with the king's divorce.

Henry the Eighth had married Catherine, his brother's widow, daughter of Ferdinand and Isabella of Spain. They had lived happily together, but their marriage had been saddened by the death of their children. Child after child died in infancy; only a daughter, Mary, lived. There was no son to follow Henry on the throne. Moreover, as one child after another died, Henry began to fear that he was being punished for a marriage which many good men believed to be against the will of God. These people thought it was wrong for a man to marry his deceased brother's wife. Then Henry fell in love with a young lady of the court, named Anne Boleyn.

Thus the rights and wrongs of the matter were very complicated. It was clearly right for Henry to regret leaving the succession to the throne in such doubt that there would probably be a war between different claimants. It was clearly wrong for Henry to fall in love with Anne Boleyn. As for the divorce which he desired from Catherine, some said one thing, and some another. Anyhow, it became Wolsey's business to secure the divorce by getting the permission of the pope. And in this he failed. In the changes of power in Europe, Italy and the pope came under the rule of Spain, and the pope would not venture to do a thing so offensive to Spain as to allow the divorce of the daughter of Ferdinand and Isabella. Thus Wolsey fell into disgrace, and his chancellorship was given to Sir Thomas More.

Then Henry decided to proceed with the divorce in spite of the pope. He followed Luther's example. The pope said to Luther, "You are excommunicated; you are from henceforth forbidden to partake of the sacraments of the Church. " Luther answered, "That will make no difference to me. I shall suffer no loss by your refusal of the sacraments: they do not depend on Church approval." The pope said to Henry, " You may not be divorced. I refuse to give you my permission." Henry answered, "That will make no difference to me. You claim to be a ruler in my kingdom, and to enforce your laws, not only in the Church but in the state. I deny the claim. You are dismissed. From this day forward you are no ruler here. I do not care for your permission. I shall do precisely as I please."

Meanwhile, the Lord Chancellor had been attending, with all diligence, to the duties of his office. Every morning he sat from eight until eleven to hear cases, and every afternoon he was to be found in his house to hear petitions. Whoever had a grievance might bring it to his notice, and the poorer the suppliant the better. In a day when the taking of bribes was a common sin of judges, More declined all gifts. One time, his enemies, —for a great man in that age always had enemies,—declared that he had received a "fair great gilt cup" from a man in whose favor he had decided a case. And More confessed that the man's wife brought him the golden cup as a New Year's gift, and that he took it.

"There, gentlemen," cried the chief accuser, "did I not tell you that you should find this matter true?" Thereupon More answered that having received the cup at the lady's hands, he caused his butler to fill it with wine, and drank to her good health, and gave it back. "Thus was this great mountain turned scarce unto a mole-hill."

One time, the Duke of Norfolk, coming to dine with the Lord Chancellor, found him at the parish church in the midst of the service, with a surplice on his back, singing in the choir. After the service, as they went home arm in arm, the Duke said, "Well, well! my Lord, a parish clerk! a parish clerk! You dishonor the king and his office."

To which the Chancellor replied, smiling, *u* Your Grace may not think that the king, your master and mine, will be offended with me for serving God, his Master."

At a little distance from his mansion house, More built a place which contained a chapel and a library; and to this building he was accustomed to go that he might be alone to read and pray; and especially on Fridays, he spent the whole day there, in his devotions, saying the seven penitential psalms and the litany and other prayers. This he found time to do, even in the midst of the great business of his high office, feeling that the essential thing, above all else, is that a man be the master of himself. And to this end, he wore under his fine clothing a shirt of hair, and sometimes flogged himself with a knotted cord, that he might exercise himself in the endurance of discomfort and pain. The devil, he said, is like an ape, who will do mischief when no one is looking, but if he is observed will leap back. Thus he kept on the watch against temptations.

In the midst, however, of all this strictness of living and this devotion to the old ways of the Church, he wrote a book called "Utopia," which was filled with the spirit of the new age. This book is in the form of an account of a strange and distant land, given to More by one who had traveled with Americus Vespucius, and in his travels had visited a people whose customs were very different from the customs of England. In this way, More was able to set forth his ideas of the right manner of living. Among other things, he said that, in Utopia, religion was free. No man there was punished for his belief, but every man might be of what religion he pleased, and might endeavor to draw others to it by the force of argument, and by amicable and honest ways, but without bitterness against those of other opinions. This seemed to be in accord with the new liberty which Luther was bringing into the Church.

Meanwhile, the matter of the king's divorce was coming forward. More was against it. He believed that the pope was right in refusing to allow it. When he perceived that the matter was decided, he resigned his office. Out he went from his high place, a poor man as he had entered it. He called his children and his grandchildren together, who were all living with him in his great house, and said that he must now reduce his expenses.

"I have been brought up," he said, "at Oxford, at an Inn of Chancery, at Lincoln's Inn, and in the King's Court. Thus I have gone from the lowest degree to the highest. Now we must go back. We will begin with Lincoln's Inn diet, and live like the prosperous lawyers; and the next year, if we are not able to maintain this, we will go one step down to the Town Inn fare, and live like the less prosperous lawyers. If that exceed our ability too, then will we the next year after descend to Oxford fare, and live like scholars. Which, if our ability stretch not to maintain neither, then may we yet, with bags and wallets, go a-begging together, and so still keep company merrily." Thus did he take his change of fortune with all cheerfulness.

While he was Lord Chancellor, one of his gentlemen, when the church service was over, was accustomed to go to his wife's pew, and say, "Madam, my Lord is gone," and thus escort her from the church. The day after he resigned his office, Sir Thomas himself came down after the service and standing by the pew made a low bow, saying, "Madam, my Lord is gone."

The king, however, was not contented with More's resignation. Chancellor or not, More was the greatest man in England, and his silence meant that he did not approve of the king's conduct. He refused to attend the coronation of Anne Boleyn. It was plain that he was opposed to the king's marriage. Thus he made an enemy of Anne and of the king. One time, he asked his daughter how Queen Anne did, and how things went at court. She answered, "Never better; there is nothing else but dancing and sporting." "Alas, Meg," said More, "it pitieth me to remember to what misery, poor soul, she will shortly come." Some say that he added, "These dances of hers will prove such dances that she will spurn off our heads like footballs."

Then the Act of Supremacy was passed, declaring the king head of the Church in England, in the pope's place. And first the clergy, and then the great men of the realm, were called upon to accept it.

"Mr. More," said the Duke of Norfolk, his good friend, "it is perilous striving with princes, and therefore I would wish you to incline somewhat to the king's pleasure."

"Is that all, my Lord?" said More. "Is there, in good faith, no more difference between your Grace and me, but that I shall die to-day and you to-morrow?"

Thus he went to appear before the Lords at Lambeth. That morning, as his custom was when he entered into any matter of importance, he went first to church and said his prayers. It was also his custom, whenever he went away from home, to have his wife and children come with him to his boat, and there to kiss them all and bid them farewell; but that morning he would not let them come, but shut the gate behind him.

Presently, in the boat, he said to William Roper, " Son Roper, I thank the Lord, the field is won."

Roper answered, "Sir, I am thereof very glad."

But as he considered what More meant, it became plain that he had thanked the Lord that He had enabled him to go forward in obedience to what his conscience called him to do, in spite of his great love of his family. When he shut the gate, he knew that for conscience' sake he was shutting himself out from his pleasant home, from all the joys of his delightful life, and from the sight of the loved faces of his wife and children.

Thus More refused to take the oath of supremacy as against his conscience, and they put him in prison in the Tower. There he remained for more than a year, in the hardship of close confinement, deprived of even books and paper.

One time, when his wife came to see him, being a simple person, and not understanding these great matters, she remonstrated with him. "What the good year, Mr. More," said she, " I marvel that you, that have been always hereunto taken for so wise a man, will now so play the fool to lie here in this close, filthy prison, and be content to be shut up among mice and rats, when you might be abroad at your liberty, and with the favor and good-will both of the king and his Council, if you would but do as all the bishops and best learned of this Realm have done. And seeing you have at Chelsea a right, fair house, your library, your books, your gallery, your garden, your orchards, where you might, in the company of me your wife, your children, and household, be merry, I muse what in God's name you mean here still fondly to tarry."

To whom Sir Thomas, having listened quietly with a cheerful countenance said, "I pray thee, tell me, tell me one thing."

"What is that?" said she.

"Is not this house as nigh heaven as mine own?"

To whom she, after her accustomed fashion, not liking much talk, answered, "Tilly vally, tilly vally!"

But his daughter Margaret understood him better. With her he said the psalms and the litany, as he had been wont to do at family prayers at home. "I find no cause, I thank God, Meg," he said, "to reckon myself in worse case here, than in mine own house" And Margaret's husband, William Roper, writing the story of his life, adds this comment, "Thus by his gracious demeanor in tribulations appeared it, that all the troubles that ever chanced unto him, by his patient sufferance thereof were to him no painful punishments, but of his patience profitable exercises."

At last, being brought to trial, the solicitor-general, Rich, recounted a conversation which he claimed to have had with More.

"Admit that there were, sir, an Act of Parliament, that all the Realm should take me for the king, would not you, Mr. More, take me for the king?"

"Yes, sir," said More, "that would I."

"I put the case further, that there were an Act of Parliament that all the Realm should take me for the pope, would then not you, Mr. More, take me for the pope?"

"For answer," said Sir Thomas, "to your first case, the Parliament may well, Mr. Rich, meddle with the state of temporal princes; but to make answer to your second case, I will put you this case: Suppose the Parliament would make a law, that God should not be God, would you then, Mr. Rich, say God were not God?"

"No, sir," said he, "that would I not, since no Parliament may make any such law."

"No more," said Sir Thomas, according to Rich's report, "could the Parliament make the king the supreme head of the Church."

This was the sole evidence against him, and this More denied. But his death had been determined. The king was not willing that there should live, even in silence, a man whose disapproval was a constant criticism upon him.

Thus he was condemned to die. And as he came, after his condemnation, from Westminster to the Tower, his daughter Margaret was waiting by the way to see him. And she, "pressing in amongst the midst of the throng and the company of the guard, that with halberds and bills were round about him, hastily ran to him, and there, openly in the sight of them all, embraced and took him about the neck and kissed him, who, well liking her most daughterly love and affection towards him, gave her his fatherly blessing, and many godly words of comfort besides; from whom after she was departed, she not satisfied with the former sight of her dear father, having respect neither to herself, nor to the press of the people and multitudes that were about him, suddenly turned back again, and ran to him as before, took him about the neck, and divers times together most lovingly kissed him, and at last with a full heavy heart was fain to depart from him; the beholding whereof was, to many of them that were present thereat, so lamentable, that it made them for very sorrow to mourn and weep."

Sir Thomas More was beheaded on the seventh day of July, 1535. The scaffold was poorly built, and as he and the lieutenant of the Tower climbed the steps together, he said, "I pray you, I pray you, Mr. Lieutenant, see me safe up, and for my coming down, let me shift for myself." Thus he died, composed and with a cheerful face, kneeling down and commending his soul to God in whom he put his trust, and whose obedience he valued above all the pleasures of his life.

When the Emperor Charles heard of this tragedy, he called the English ambassador, and said, "My Lord Ambassador, we understand that the king, your master, hath put his faithful servant and grave wise councilor, Sir Thomas More, to death." The ambassador answered that the circumstances were unknown to him. "Well," said the emperor, "it is very true, and this we will say, that if we had been master of such a servant, we would rather have lost the best city of our dominions, than such a worthy councilor."

LOYOLA
1491-1556

The armies of France and Spain were fighting for the town of Pampeluna. The Spaniards were within, holding the place; the French were without, attacking it. Most of the garrison wished to surrender, being few in number and the enemy very strong; but they were restrained by a young knight named Ignatius of Loyola. The French, accordingly, assaulted the walls, and in the battle a cannon ball wounded Ignatius in both his legs. With his fall, the day was lost, and the French took the city. They were kind to the knight, whose bravery they admired, and carried him to his own home near by, that he might be cured of his hurt, and the war went on. The incident attracted no particular attention. Nevertheless, it was the most important thing which had happened in Europe since the thunderstorm which terrified Luther, and made him resolve to enter a monastery.

The cannon ball changed the whole course of young Loyola's life. He had been a merry lad, whose chief desire in life was to enjoy the world. At home, in his father's castle, he had had the company of twelve brothers and sisters, he being the thirteenth and the youngest of the family. Then he had gone, as the custom was, to be a page at the court of Ferdinand and Isabella, where he behaved like other such young gallants of that time, dancing with the ladies, fighting and gambling with the men. Now he could dance no more. His leg had been badly set and had to be broken over again before the doctors could make it straight. Even then a bone protruded below the knee. When Loyola saw it, and realized that it would spoil the smoothness of his silk stocking, he ordered it sawed off. All this he endured without a groan, showing his pain only by the clenching of his fists. The shock, however, was so great that he fell into a sickness from which he seemed unlikely to recover. But the crisis passed, and there he lay, slowly regaining strength. It was plain that he could no longer live the gay life of a knight.

During the long weeks of his recovery he read two books, for lack of other occupation. He asked for novels, but there were none in the house. The best they could do was to bring him a Life of Christ, and a volume of brief biographies, called the "Flowers of the Saints." These he read, idly at first, often looking up and thinking of a certain young lady of the court, how he would presently see her again, and what he would say and do on that happy occasion, and so putting the book down. But gradually he became interested. He saw that the saints of the book were knights like the heroes of the romances, only they fought in a different war and in a different way. He saw that they did deeds of great danger with high courage, and that they suffered pain as if they liked it. The young knight said to himself, "What if I should do what St. Francis did?" "What if I should do what St. Dominic did?"

There was not, at first, much religion in these thoughts. Loyola's ambition was stirred to see if he could not endure hardness as well as these saints had endured it. He noticed, however, that his thoughts made a difference in him. When he thought of the court, and the gaieties of the life there, he felt pleasure for the moment, but was afterwards depressed and sad. But when he thought of the saints, and planned to go on difficult pilgrimages, and to starve and scourge himself, he was conscious of a deep and continuing refreshment of spirit. This led him to watch his mind, and to note the effect of different thoughts. He perceived that his spiritual condition depended, not only on doing right, but on thinking right. It was like the discovery of a new medicine. He began to apply it to himself, and then to others, practising what he afterwards called "spiritual exercises."

As soon as he was well again, he set out to go to Montserrat, where there was a great Benedictine monastery. On the way he was joined by a Moor, who was traveling in the same direction; for the Moors, who were of the religion of Mohammed, were still in great numbers in Spain. Loyola and the Moor talked together as they journeyed, and the conversation led on into theology, and they held a stout debate, in which the Christian, for lack of education and training, was worsted. Then they came to a place where a path turned from the main road to the monastery. On went the Moor, leaving Loyola defeated and distressed. At last he said, all his knightly impulses urging him, "I have lost one battle, but I will try another. I will ride after this Moor and kill him." Then he remembered the brotherly love of the saints whose lives he had been reading. Being perplexed what to do, he left it to the horse, and the horse happily took the road which ran to Montserrat.

Stopping in a village by the way, the pilgrim bought a piece of sackcloth, filled with prickly wooden fibers, which he made into a garment long enough to reach to his feet. He bought also a pair of shoes such as the poorest people wore. To these he added a pilgrim's staff, and a gourd such as pilgrims carried to drink from. He tied his purchases to his saddle, and rode on.

Arriving at the monastery, he made a confession of all the sins which he could remember to have committed during his whole life. Then, like a knight, before a quest, he hung his sword before an altar of the Blessed Virgin, and kept a vigil, praying unceasingly till morning. That, he knew, was what Amadis de Gaul would have done, the favorite hero of the romances of chivalry. His horse he had given to the monastery; his fine clothes he had given to a beggar. Dressed in sackcloth, he walked in his rough shoes to the town of Manresa, where he found lodging in a Dominican convent. There he daily prayed and fasted and scourged himself. Once he went for a week without tasting food. He was trying to do what the saints in the books had done. Taking the old theory of the saints that the body is a vile and evil thing, and that we ought to pay no heed to it except to torment it, he ceased to comb his hair and to wash his hands. He was greatly troubled at this time about his past sins, trying to remember some which he had perhaps forgotten. Back and forth he went over his life, as one who searches the way for a lost coin, seeking for a lost sin.

Out of this condition he was brought, partly by the advice of a good friend, and partly by the instincts of his own nature; two ways whereby God speaks to men. His adviser counseled him to let past things be past, and to trouble himself no more about them. His common sense taught him that the best thing he could do with his life was to use it, like a good knight, for the good of others; he would tell his neighbors that secret of right thinking which he had learned for himself. It was plain, therefore, that he could not be a hermit, living in a cave; neither could he be an ascetic, so neglectful of his body and his clothing that people would hate the sight of him. Already, he began to get a dim vision of a new kind of sainthood, among men, in the active world.

Starting out from Manresa, Ignatius Loyola begged his way to Rome, and thence to Venice, and thence by ship to Jerusalem. There he intended to remain, saying his prayers daily at the holy places, and helping pilgrims. The Franciscans, however, who were in charge of the Christian services in Jerusalem, discouraged him, partly because they were too poor to add another beggar to their family, and partly because they were afraid that Loyola, by his zeal, would anger the Turks.

It was now clear to Loyola that God intended him to save souls. He was to be neither a hermit, nor a monk, nor a pilgrim, but a teacher of religion. He was to be a physician of the spirit. It was the wise rule of the Church, however, that nobody should undertake the cure of souls until he had prepared himself by careful study. So Loyola went to school. He settled down at Barcelona and began taking lessons in Latin grammar. It was very hard for him, being now thirty-three years of age, and having spent his life thus far in the pleasures of the court, in the excitements of war, in spiritual combats, and in the adventures of a journey to the East; and having always in his mind the secret process of the spiritual exercises by which he hoped to convert the world. He tried hard, but, for a long time, in vain, to commit the declensions and conjugations to memory. He could not keep his attention on his books. Two years of effort, however, made a difference in his habits of mind, and he was advanced enough to go to Alcala, where there was a university.

At Alcala he began to teach privately. He was like one who had discovered a wonderful medicine, and who cannot wait until he has been made a doctor. He tried the spiritual exercises on his fellow stu dents, and presently gathered such crowds about him that the Church, fearing the effects of the teaching of such an imperfectly educated person, put him in prison, and then, after some months, setting him free, forbade him to teach again till he had studied four years more.

Leaving Alcala, after this treatment, he went to another university, at Salamanca. There again he was imprisoned as a dangerous person. He and a companion were chained foot to foot, and fastened to a stake. The Church authorities, in those days, were very nervous on account of the new ideas of Luther. They were afraid that Loyola was a heretic. Nothing, however, was proved against him, but he was again forbidden to teach till after four years' preparation. All this he endured with patience, making no complaint, but on his release, he went to still another university, in Paris. There again he came under suspicion of the authorities, but he continued his studies, fighting hard with inattention and with the sickness which frequently beset him, and gathering about him a little group of kindred spirits.

At Paris, he began his lessons over again, and entered a class of boys. He hated to study, but compelled himself to it. One time, he said to himself, "I will think of the master as Christ, and will obey him as I would obey Christ." Thus, as he had already overcome the temptations of his body, he now overcame the temptations of his mind. In 1534, having completed his studies, he was given the degree of Master of Arts. He had learned also the supreme art of conquering himself.

In that year a group of seven young men met in a church in Paris, and under the leadership of Loyola, solemnly devoted themselves to the work of the ministry, according to the new way which he had discovered. They were like a group of young doctors devoting themselves to a new way of practising medicine. They resolved to meet again after a time in Venice, and thence to go on a pilgrimage to Jerusalem, or, in case that was found impossible, to offer their services to the pope. The Jerusalem journey had to be given up, and in 1537 the companions were in Rome. There they were ordained to the priesthood. And there they formed themselves into a society, which Loyola named the Company of Jesus. In 1540, the society was formally recognized by the pope, and Loyola was unanimously chosen its first general.

The method of the new society was set forth in the Spiritual Exercises. It was a new way of dealing with the soul. Loyola had found it a cure for his sins, and had devoted himself to applying it to the sins of his neighbors. One time, being in the house of a friendly nobleman, he had been invited to join him in a game of billiards, but the custom was to play for some stake, and Loyola, being a poor student, had no money. So he said, "If you win, I will be your servant for a month; but if I win you shall be my servant for a month." So they played, and Loyola won. And he made the nobleman go through the Spiritual Exercises, at the end of which he was a converted man, filled with penitence and faith, and resolved to live a better life. It is an illustration of the way in which the founder of the Company of Jesus lost no opportunity to put his ideas into practice.

Loyola made the Spiritual Exercises into a book, a drill-book of the soul. It was intended to make saints, as a military drill-book is intended to make soldiers. It became the most influential book in Europe. It changed the lives of multitudes of men. It dealt with sin as a disease, and cured sinners. One of the strong arguments of Luther against the Church of that day was the immorality of priests and people. No honest person could deny that there was urgent need of a Reformation. The only question was whether this reform should be conducted outside or inside the Church. Luther went out, and summoned all good people to follow him. But Loyola's plan was to reform the Church from within. The result of it was to establish a counterreformation. It was Ignatius Loyola, more than any other man, who kept Spain and Italy and France from following Germany and England in their religious revolutions. He saved the Roman Church. /

This he did by the medicine of the Spiritual Exercises. Loyola had found in his own experience that human nature is profoundly affected by the act of thinking. Our thoughts make a difference in our lives. What the sinner needs, therefore, in order to overcome his sins is to think steadily and continuously for a good while about truth and right. Thus Loyola arranged a series of meditations to cover the space of four weeks. During the first week the thoughts were directed to the consideration of sin, death, judgment, and hell. The subject in the second week was the Kingdom of Christ, and the soul's choice of the service of God. In the third week the thoughts were fixed upon the passion and death of Jesus, and in the fourth week, upon His resurrection.

In order to make these meditations the more effective, the patient must withdraw from the world during these twenty-eight days, and put himself in charge of a director. It is like going to a hospital and putting oneself in the care of a physician. The director examines the penitent regularly and often, and prescribes what is to be done.

Each meditation begins with an act of imagination. The penitent is to take some incident of the Gospel, or some such fact as death or hell, and make it real to all his senses. He is "to *see* the vast fires of hell, and the souls inclosed in certain fiery bodies, as it were in dungeons; and to *hear* the lamentations, the hardships, the exclamations, the blasphemies against Christ and His Saints, thence break forth; and to perceive by the *smell* also of the imagination the smoke, the brimstone, and the stench of a kind of stink or filth, and of putrefaction; and to *taste* in like manner those most bitter things, as the tears, the rottenness, and the worm of conscience; and to *touch* in a manner those fires, by the touch of which their souls themselves are burnt."

Each meditation ends with a conversation between the penitent and Christ or the Virgin Mary, full of resolution and affection.

Sometimes the four weeks were lengthened into six; sometimes they were shortened; but the idea was that for most persons a course of twenty-eight days would be sufficient to rid them effectually of all sin and doubt. Each penitent began in the solitude and absolute stillness of a darkened room, and when, near the end, amidst thoughts of the resurrection, the shutters were opened, and the sun streamed in, the sun of righteousness was expected to have dawned in the soul.

A further condition of success was a giving up of the will of the penitent to the will of the director. All directions must be followed without delay or question. This became a general principle of the new society. Nobody could enter it except by the initiation of the Spiritual Exercises, and the effect of the exercises was to exalt the virtue of obedience. The Jesuit was to have no more mind of his own than a dead body. He was to do what his superior commanded him, and all superiors were to obey the general of the order.

Thus Loyola brought into being a society which was unlike any other. Benedict, long before, had brought men together to live under a religious rule in monasteries. Francis and Dominic had sent them out from their prayers to preach to the people, but they carried the monastery on their backs, being dressed in garments which showed at once what manner of men they were. Ignatius Loyola prescribed for his companions only the ordinary dress of a clergyman. They were to go into the world freely, to be ministers of parishes, to be professors in colleges, to gain the confidence and so direct the plans of princes. They were to use all possible means of influence. They were to bring to the help of souls the Spiritual Exercises which they practised themselves, and they were to live under the rule of immediate obedience.

It is easy to see how such a society aroused the suspicion and dislike, not only of Protestants, but of Catholics. It was a secret society: nobody knew who belonged to it. Making its way unobserved into politics and education, and having the strength which comes with unquestioning obedience to the word of command, the Company of Jesus alarmed Europe. The Jesuits were blamed for teaching these evil doctrines: the doctrine of probabilism, which means that if you can find an act commended of any writer of repute, you may assume that it is right, and do it with a clear conscience; the doctrine of mental reservation, which means that you may say one thing aloud, and another and very different thing under your breath; and the doctrine that the end justifies the means, so that if the main purpose is to do a good thing, for the glory of God and the welfare of the Church, and a lie will help, you may lie, and not be blamed. The Jesuits said that these were slanders. It is certain that they had no place in the life of Loyola. It is certain also that Jesuit fathers, in India on the one side, and in Canada on the other, among the savages, showed a missionary zeal, and a courage in facing dangers and death, which have never been surpassed in all the records of martyrdom.

CRANMER
1489-1556
The divorce of Henry the Eighth, which made Thomas More a martyr, made Thomas Cranmer an archbishop.

Cranmer was a professor in the University of Cambridge. He was a quiet man, well liked by those who knew him, a pleasant person, a student, fond of books, fond also of hunting, and of riding difficult horses. "He was a slow reader," says one of his biographers, "but a diligent marker of whatsoever he read; for he seldom read without pen in hand, and whatsoever made for either one part or the other of things being in controversy, he wrote it out if it were short, or, at least, noted the author and the place, that he might find it and write it out by leisure." 74 THOMAS CRAXMER
From the Painting by G. Fliccius in the National Portrait Gallery

This habit of considering both sides of matters in dispute was characteristic of him, and was of large importance when he became a leader of the English Reformation; though it brought him into many troubles. It has caused him to be misunderstood ever since by those who wish their heroes to be not only upright but downright, with no uncertainty. Cranmer was like More in his sympathy with both sides. They differed in that More inclined on the whole to the old ways, but Cranmer to the new.

Cranmer would have been contented to live out all his life, reading and lecturing, studying the Bible and teaching it, taking no part in the commotions of the great world. But, one summer, the plague came to Cambridge, and closed the university, driving everybody out; and Cranmer went to stay with two of his pupils at Waltham, in the country. At the same time, the king, with some of his chief officers, was making a visit in that neighborhood, and two of the great men were lodged in the hospitable house in which Cranmer was staying. They were old Cambridge men, acquaintances of Cranmer's, and meeting thus at dinner they naturally fell to talking about the matter which all England was discussing, the question of the king's divorce.

Not only was that question undecided, but there seemed to be no speedy prospect of decision. According to the general opinion of the time, the proper person to decide it was the pope. It was a pope who had permitted Henry, twenty years before, to marry his brother's widow; if that permission was wrong, and against the will of God, as some said, it ought to be reversed in the Pope's Court. But the pope was in a difficult position. France and Spain were fighting over Italy. Whichever won became, by his victory, the master of the pope. At first, the French were victorious, and the pope sent word to England that Cardinal Wolsey might try the case; knowing, of course, that Wolsey would decide against Catherine. But then the Spaniards overcame the French, and the pope sent another word to Wolsey to stop him; for Catherine was the conquering emperor's aunt. The king's matter was postponed and postponed; and his anger was increased by the fact that the pope dared to say only what the king of France or the king of Spain, whichever was in power, told him to say. Thus the interests of England, so far as they depended on the pope, depended really on the courts of France or Spain to which he was in subjection. The king of Spain was thus able to say to the king of England, "You may not be divorced. I will not permit it. I will tell the pope to prevent you." It was not only the pope's refusal of the divorce which made Henry reject the papacy, but the fact that, under the political circumstances, obedience to the pope meant obedience to the king of Spain, his master.

Thus Cranmer and Fox and Gardiner sat about the table after dinner, discussing this situation. And the Cambridge professor made a new suggestion. Why depend, he said, upon the judgment of the pope? This is a matter of plain right and wrong. If the king's marriage was illegal, according to the teaching of the Bible and the law of the Church, then it was illegal, and that is the end of it. Why not submit the question to learned men who understand the Bible and the law? They are likely to know better than the pope. Why not refer the matter to the Christian universities of England and Europe?

This suggestion was reported to the king, and there is a tradition that he said, "I will speak to him. Let him be sent for out of hand. This man, I trow, has got the right sow by the ear." Cranmer was brought to the king, and ordered to set down his ideas in writing. He returned to the university no more. He entered into the service of the king.

Cranmer's plan was tried, but without much success. The universities were asked to say whether, in their opinion, the king might properly put away his wife. Some of the learned men were very prudent and would not risk the king's displeasure; some were bribed, some were compelled. It was plain, however, that the true judgment of wise men was against the king. At last, Henry took the matter into his own hands. He declared his independence of the pope. The case should be decided, not in Italy, but in England. And the man who should decide it was Thomas Cranmer himself.

For the king had found, in Cranmer, a man after his own heart. He had advanced him from one position to another. He had sent him as ambassador to Rome; he had sent him as ambassador to Germany. In 1533, only four years after the conference between the professor and the king at Waltham, Cranmer had become Archbishop of Canterbury. He summoned the queen to appear before him, and when she refused he declared her marriage null and void. He sanctioned the marriage between Henry and Anne; he crowned Anne as queen of England.

Our sympathy in this matter is against the archbishop and the king. We feel that Cranmer was neither saint nor hero. It must be remembered, however, that the situation was confused and difficult. There were good men who honestly believed that the only hope for England, both as a church and as a nation, lay in making the king independent of the pope. There were good men who believed also that the king had had no right to marry his brother's widow, and that his union with Catherine ought to be dissolved. Cranmer was one of these.

For good or ill, the thing was done. In 1535, Parliament declared that the king "justly and rightfully is, and ought to be, the Supreme Head of the Church of England." The authority of the pope was ended. In the place of the Papal Supremacy there was now a Royal Supremacy. The king had all power in his hands. One after another, he struck down all possible resistance. The monasteries were on the side of the pope. Henry put them on trial; proved to his satisfaction that the friars of St. Francis and St. Dominic were only idle beggars, and the monks of St. Benedict and St. Bernard were only selfish landowners, caring for nothing but ease and money; turned them all out, pulled down their houses, and took most of their treasures to enrich himself and his friends. The Church was, for the most part, on the side of the pope. Henry directed what ceremonies should be used and what disused, and what should be believed and disbelieved, and told the preachers what to preach. Many of the great nobles were against these changes; Henry cut off their heads, beginning with Sir Thomas More. As for the people, they dared not speak. The Parliament obeyed the king. The land lay under a reign of terror.

Cranmer, always a gentle and submissive person, stood as far apart from all this as he dared. Twice he ventured to speak. Once to beg for the pardon of Anne Boleyn, again to beg for the pardon of Thomas Cromwell, the king's righthand in all this business, when these two evil spirits of Henry's reign had fallen from their high estate and were under sentence of death. He was, indeed, archbishop, the last archbiship under the pope, the first under the king. But the conditions were such that even a man like Becket could have accomplished nothing. Cranmer was very unlike Becket: a Cambridge professor, a man of books, brought against his will into the midst of all these fierce commotions.

In one matter Cranmer was successful. He was able to get the Bible in English into the hands of the people.

Wycliffe's translation of the Bible was by this time hard to read; because, since his day, the English language had changed. There were many different words and different spellings. William Tyndale had therefore taken in hand the work of translating the Bible into the English which people actually spoke. This he had done for the New Testament and for the Old Testament through the historical books, making practically the Bible, thus far, which we read today. But Tyndale's Bibles had been burned in England, and he himself had been put to death. This was largely because he had filled the margins of his Bible with notes in which he attacked the Church and pointed out the errors of the pope. This was before Henry had begun his quarrel. That quarrel once being begun, it was plain to Henry and his advisers that an English Bible in the hands of the people would be a reinforcement to his side. In the meantime, Miles Coverdale had translated the poetical and prophetical books of the Old Testament, which Tyndale had left untranslated, and John Rogers had put Tyndale's work and Coverdale's together. This Bible, at Cranmer's suggestion, was put in all the churches.

Otherwise, the Reformation in England stopped short at the expulsion of the pope. The king was never a Protestant, and as the years went by he was less and less disposed to favor Protestant ideas. But he liked Cranmer. The men of the Old Learning hated Cranmer. They suspected him, with good reason, of being in sympathy with the changes in ceremonies and in beliefs which were taking place in Germany.

One time, they drew up a solemn accusation against the archbishop and presented it to the king. A few days later, Henry was in his boat on the river, and was being rowed past Lambeth, where Cranmer lived, and there was Cranmer standing by the water on the steps. The king called him to come and sit beside him. "Ha," said the king, "I have news for you: I know now who is the greatest heretic in Kent!" And he pulled out the paper which Bishop Gardiner and the others had written. Cranmer asked to have a commission appointed to give him a fair trial. "That will I do," said the king, "I will appoint a commission, and the head of it shall be yourself, and the others shall be such as you may choose! And your commission shall examine these brethren and their plot against their archbishop."

Another time, the Council demanded that Cranmer should be imprisoned in the Tower. Late that night, Henry sent for the archbishop and told him. Cranmer said that he was willing to go to prison, if he might be fairly tried. "No, not so, my Lord," said the king. "I have better regard unto you than to permit your enemies to overthrow you. Go to the Council when they call you, and require them to bring forward your accusers. Then if they refuse, and command that you be imprisoned, show them this ring." And the king gave Cranmer the ring which meant that whatever matter was in dispute must be immediately referred to him. So the Council met, and sent for the archbishop, and kept him waiting for half an hour outside the door, intending to insult him. When they let him in they accused him of poisoning the minds of the people with heresy. To the Tower he must go. Then Cranmer showed them the king's ring. At once, the meeting was broken up, and they all went, pale and trembling, to the king. "Ah, my Lords," he cried, "I had thought that I had a discreet and wise Council, but now I perceive that I am deceived. I would you would well understand that I account my Lord of Canterbury as faithful a man toward me as ever was prelate in this realm, and one to whom I am many ways beholden by the faith I owe to God; and therefore whoso loveth me will regard him hereafter."

One step Cranmer was able to take toward that translation and revision of the services of the Church which was his greatest contribution to religion. In 1545 there appeared by the king's permission a primer for the use of the people; that is, a book containing the Creed, the Lord's Prayer, and the Ten Commandments in English, together with simple instructions in faith and conduct; and in the primer was a litany in English. It was the Latin litany, to which the people were accustomed, translated and improved. Made out of old materials, and keeping the responses which had long been used, it was put into the language of the nation, into sentences so stately that no English writing has ever surpassed them, by the hand of Cranmer. This is the litany which still stands in the Book of Common Prayer.

Then Henry the Eighth died, holding Cranmer's hand, and Edward the Sixth reigned in his stead.

Edward was only nine years old, and the government of England came into the hand of great nobles, first Somerset, then Northumberland. With these ambitious men the Reformation was a matter of politics rather than of religion. What they wanted was such a compromise between the old learning and the new as should continue them in power. In Somerset's time the compromise favored the old ways; the purpose was to reform the Church, but not to make such changes as to drive the conservative people out. In Northumberland's time, the compromise favored the new ways; changes were made more freely. Under these conditions Cranmer put forth two prayer-books, one in 1549, the other in 1552. His own disposition was in agreement with the temper of the time. He believed in compromise. He desired to keep all good people in the Church of England. At the same time, his own beliefs were slowly changing from the old doctrines to the new. All this appears in the two books. He did not have a free hand like Luther in Wittenberg or Calvin in Geneva. He was the chief officer of a church which had exchanged the authority of the pope for the authority of the king. He had to do what the king's representatives told him to do. His work had to be done in conference with committees and submitted to Parliament. Still, the two books were for the most part made by him, and bear the impression of his genius.

The first book was translated from the ancient forms of the missal and the breviary, and differed from them mainly in being in English instead of Latin, and in being shortened and simplified. The services, which had been so complicated that only priests and monks could follow them, were now adapted to the use of all the people. The first book was revised to make the second by little changes here and there, to commend it to the favor of reformers. Thus in 1549, the priest, when he gave the bread to the people in the Holy Communion, said, "The Body of our Lord Jesus Christ"; that seemed to be in accordance with the doctrine of the Middle Ages. But in 1552, he was in structed to say, "Take and eat this in remembrance," and that seemed to be in accordance with the doctrine of the Reformation.

The second book had hardly appeared before the young king came to the end of his short life, and Mary, the daughter of the queen whom Henry had divorced, came to the throne.

At once, the whole face of affairs was changed. The progress of the Reformation was sharply checked. The men who had been prominent in religion in the days of Edward, began to run away. Bishops and deans, doctors of divinity and preachers, fled across the English Channel for their lives. Cranmer remained. Inclined as he was to compromise, and to see truth on both sides, gentle and humbleminded and retiring, he was no coward. He made a public declaration of his belief that "all the doctrine and religion set forth by our sovereign lord, King Edward VI., is more pure and according to God's word than any other that hath been used in England for these thousand years." He was immediately committed to the Tower, and was imprisoned in the cell from which Northumberland had just been taken to execution.

The great offense of Cranmer was his part in the divorce of Catherine. Her daughter could not forgive it. But Mary was not only Catherine's daughter but a zealous believer in the old ways. She hated the Reformation and everything connected with it. The former customs were restored. The use of the English prayer-book was forbidden. The Latin mass came back. England submitted to the pope. There was no place in the nation for a Protestant archbishop. Parliament passed an act of persecution, making it lawful to burn heretics. And the burning began. Within six months fifty eminent and devout men, some of them being bishops, had perished at the stake. Cranmer himself saw Bishop Ridley and Bishop Latimer burned alive in Oxford beside the wall of Balliol College. "Be of good cheer, Master Ridley," cried Latimer. "Be of good cheer, and play the man, for we shall light this day such a candle in England as by the grace of God shall never be put out."

Cranmer was held for further trial. He was kept in prison, where he lay for two years. He was subjected, sometimes to arguments, sometimes to threats, sometimes to promises. The purpose, from the beginning, was to kill him, but there was hope that he might be tricked into a denial of the principles of the Reformation. Then the pope and the queen would have the satisfaction, not only of burning the leader of the reforming movement, but of condemning the movement by his own words. And the trick succeeded. After his long imprisonment, they succeeded in working upon his belief, which he held in common with most people of his time, that the royal authority was the voice of God: "the powers that be," as St. Paul said, "are ordained of God." Queen Mary, then, must be obeyed. There he was alone; all his friends were fled across the sea; only his enemies were about him. Many matters which are now clear to us were very confused then. He saw also that amongst all the wrongs of the old ways there was much which was right; and that the reformers had made some mistakes. His mind was curiously modern in his perception of the fact that only the ignorant may honestly claim that they know everything. Thus they overbore him, and he signed what they gave him to sign.

But one thing remained. He was to be burned to death, but before that, he was to be brought to Church in the presence of the people. He had been imprisoned in Oxford, and this last scene was in St. Mary's Church. There he stood on a platform opposite the pulpit, and listened to a sermon. Curiously, the preacher comforted the martyr by reminding him how the three Hebrews of the old time, refusing to worship the idols of a wicked king, had passed unharmed through the burning, fiery furnace. Then all knelt for prayers, and when the prayers were ended, Cranmer arose. He began to declare what he believed. "Now," he said, "I come to the great thing that so troubleth my conscience more than any other thing that I said or did in my life: and that is my setting abroad of writings contrary to the truth, which here now I renounce and refuse as things written with my hand contrary to the truth which I thought in my heart and written for fear of death, and to save my life, if it might be; and that is all such bills as I have written or signed with mine own hand since my degradation. And forasmuch as my hand offended in writing contrary to my heart, it shall first be burned. And as for the pope, I refuse him as Christ's enemy and AntiChrist, with all his false doctrines. And as for the Sacrament "But here his enemies rose up with a great cry and tumult, and stopped him. He was dragged out of the Church to the place where Ridley and Latimer had suffered. As the flames arose around him, he said, with a loud voice, "This hand hath offended," and held it steadily in the fire. Thus he died a martyr for Christ and the Church, true to the convictions of his conscience.

There is an evident difference between bravery and boldness. The bold man, having a stout will, a natural inclination to fight, and an absolutely clear conviction that all the right is on his side, does not know what fear is. The brave man, humbly doubting his own wisdom, anxious to do right, now advancing and now retreating as he makes his difficult way, and horribly, afraid, gains at last the victory over his fears. Trembling, he compels himself to go on. This battle, Cranmer fought and won.

He was, indeed, unlike St. Michael in the pictures, who, without a sign of struggle, his face serene, and not a feather ruffled in his wings, holds the defeated devil down. He resembled Thomas, the apostle whose name he bore, who, after painful difficulties of disbelief, cried, " My Lord and my God!" The fact that he failed, and only through failure succeeded, makes him one of the most human and appealing of the English saints.

CALVIN
1509-1564

WHEN Luther nailed the theses to the door of the Wittenberg Church, John Calvin was only eight years old.

In the town of Noyon, where he lived, in France, the greatest person was the bishop, and Calvin's father was the bishop's secretary. It was his father's intention that the lad should be a priest. When he was twelve years old, he was appointed chaplain in the cathedral. At the age of eighteen, he was made the curate of a neighboring parish, and this curacy was changed for a better when he was twenty. In his new parish, he preached several sermons, but his chief duty was to draw his salary. He had not been ordained, and these pleasant appointments were according to those curious ar 98 rangements of the time by which church positions were given to laymen, and even to children, for the sake of the money. Somebody else, at a much smaller salary, did the work.

This was one of the evils of which Luther was complaining. But Luther's attacks had made little impression on the Church in France. The great rebellion which he was leading was not yet taken very seriously in that country. To be a priest seemed still a safe, comfortable, and most excellent occupation. The boy was fond of books, a good scholar, able to write and speak well, and the best debater in his class. His father's influence with the bishop would be sure to get him a fine position. Some day he might be a great bishop himself.

But something happened. Calvin's father fell out of the favor of the cathedral clergy, and Calvin, in the course of his studies, began to find that the Church in France was quite different from the Church which was described in the New Testament. It was decided that instead of being a minister, he should be a lawyer. He was sent to the University of Paris. He studied law. He was still the best scholar, and occasionally, when one of the professors was absent, he was asked to lecture. He learned, not only Latin, but Greek. He began to be interested in the new ideas which were being taught by Erasmus.

At that time, Greek was the newest thing in the world of learning. For hundreds of years, the Greeks had been forgotten. Now their statues and their books were re-discovered; and with the statues came a new vision of the glory of art, and with the books came a new way of thinking and a new way of looking at the world. It was remembered that the New Testament was written in Greek, and when Erasmus published an edition of it in its original language, men began to study it with a new interest. So narrow had been the range of knowledge that Thomas Aquinas had written a book in which he intended to include it all! Then the discoveries of Columbus had made it necessary to re-write all the old geographies, and the discoveries of Copernicus had made it necessary to re-write all the old astronomies. And Luther had begun the Reformation of the Church. It was a wonderful time, and Calvin, in Paris, found himself in the midst of it. He began to change his mind about being a lawyer. He began to interest himself in religion.

Then a friend of Calvin's, Nicholas Cop, was elected rector of the University of Paris, and in his inaugural address he declared himself frankly in favor of the new learning. He showed his agreement with the principles of the Reformation. The address made a great stir in Paris. All the conservatives arose against it. The new rector had to make his escape as best he could to save his life. Calvin also was threatened with arrest. His rooms were searched, and his books and papers seized. It was plain that a choice must be made between the old way and the new, and Calvin made it. He resigned his place as chaplain of the cathedral of Noyon, and as rector of the parish of Pont l'Eveque. He was imprisoned for a time at Noyon in consequence of an uproar in the Church, caused, probably, by outcries against him in the congregation, by those who suspected him of sympathy with the reforming movement. After this, there was no more uncertainty. John Calvin had committed himself to the cause of the Reformation.

Calvin was now twenty-five years old. He meant to be a teacher. All his interest was in study. Already he had great learning, which he now increased by reading Hebrew, but the most remarkable quality of his mind was a singular sense of order. He was not contented with his ideas until he had got them in a shape as logical and accurate as a problem in algebra. He found himself among men who had perceived new and wonderful truths in theology, and were discussing them with great enthusiasm, and following them out in many directions, but who had not succeeded in bringing them into a system. The old theology was a complete system. It had taken truth, and studied it, and worked it out into conclusions which explained everything. It was absolutely definite. It had put all things in heaven and earth into what were considered their proper places. It was like a splendidly drilled army, and the enthusiastic reformers, in attacking it, were in the position of a mob of untrained men, without discipline, attacking a regiment of regular soldiers. The mob may be right and the regiment may be wrong, but the regiment will surely win the day.

Calvin saw that the new ideas must be brought into an order as logical as the old. He took them as a drill-master takes a lot of raw recruits and makes them stand erect, and keep step, and obey the word of command. He had the genius to do it. He contributed to the Reformation the strength of a definite theology.

Calvin's chief work, the "Institutes of the Christian Religion," belongs among the supreme books. It is one of those writings which have profoundly influenced the minds and lives of men. Luther's German Bible and Cranmer's English Prayer-book brought the forces of religious thought and conduct into the midst of the people. They provided the materials of discussion and devotion. Loyola and Calvin took the spiritual forces and did with them what the man of science does when he takes steam and electricity and puts them into machines. The Spiritual Exercises applied machinery to Christian conduct. The Institutes did the same for Christian belief.

Calvin's system, however difficult to accept, is quite easy to understand.
1. God, he said, is the ruler of the world. All power is His, all wisdom and all goodness. The highest duty of every human being is to obey His will. 2. The

will of God is made known to us by the Word of God, the Bible. This is God's book, and is to be reverenced, and taken without question, and obeyed. 3. But man cannot obey God without help. For the whole human race is bad. It began good with Adam, but when he sinned, human nature became evil. Of ourselves, we can neither do, nor speak, nor think aright. We are like branches growing in a decaying tree. 4. Out of this hopeless state, Christ came to save us. This He did by offering Himself a sacrifice upon the Cross to turn away the wrath of God. 5. We lay hold of this salvation by faith. This is a union of our heart with Christ, like the grafting of a branch into a good tree. One of the consequences of faith is repentance, and another is a righteous life. 6. But some have faith and are saved, and others have not faith and are lost, according to the will of God. From all eternity, without regard to our goodness or our badness, simply of His own pleasure, He appointed some of us to salvation and others to perdition. "When it is asked why the Lord did so, we must answer, Because He pleased. But if you proceed further to ask why He pleased, you ask for something greater and more sublime than the will of God, and nothing such can be found." We were predestined to eternal life or death before the world was made.

When he had finished the writing of the Institutes, Calvin went back to France to settle up his affairs, intending to spend the rest of his life in quiet study in Basel. On his return he spent a day in Geneva. That fair city, on the lake, in sight of the perpetual snows of Mont Blanc, was in the midst of a contention between the old faith and the new. The leader of the Protestants was William Farel, an earnest man, energetic and determined, with a voice which could be heard above the noise of an angry crowd. He came to Calvin and urged him to stay in Geneva. Calvin refused; he must return, he said, to his books at Basel. But Farel insisted; he declared in his great voice that God had other work for Calvin than the quiet tasks of reading and writing. At last, Calvin consented. He said afterwards that "God had stretched forth His hand from on high" to stop him. He went to Basel, gathered his books together, and settled in Geneva.

The city was governed by the bishop, the duke, and the Syndics. The four syndics were elected annually by the citizens. They chose a company of twentyfive called the Little Council, and the Little Council chose a larger company called the Two Hundred. The three powers—the bishop, the duke, and the citizens,—were always fighting among themselves, until the duke and the bishop combined against the citizens, and the citizens rose up in might and expelled them both. This political strife against the bishop was Farel's opportunity, and he preached the doctrines of the Reformation so vigorously that the Protestants grew strong enough to seize the cathedral, drive out the Catholics, break the images, and substitute the preaching of sermons for the saying of masses. In May, 1536, the General Assembly of the citizens was called together by the sound of bells and trumpets, and they voted that they were in agreement with the Reformation. Calvin came in August.

Immediately, his influence began to appear, first over Farel, then over the whole city. He applied his clear mind, and strong will, and sense of order, to public affairs. He brought the people under discipline.

Men were appointed to inspect the conduct of the people. The city was divided into districts, each with its inspector. Every citizen who was found in fault was to be reported to one of the ministers, and if he refused to change his ways he was to be rejected from the company of Christians. It was the old excommunication in a new form.

The citizens were summoned in groups of ten, to declare their faith, whether they were Protestants or Catholics. If they were Catholics, the sooner they left the city the better.

Also in the schools, the children were to be taught a catechism, which Calvin had prepared.

Against these rigors a considerable body of citizens protested. They disliked the severity which would abolish, not only dancing and card-playing, but the keeping of Christmas and Easter. They hated the inspection, which not only called them to account for misdemeanors, but prescribed what sort of clothes they might and might not wear. They objected to the interference of the preachers with politics. They refused to be brought under rules, like school children. And the result was that the Two Hundred, after long and stormy discussions, banished Farel and Calvin from Geneva.

Calvin went to Strassburg, and resumed his studies. He occupied himself with reading and writing, he taught theology, and preached four times a week. He took much interest in arranging the services of the Church. Luther and Cranmer had made few changes in the old forms of worship. They had each translated the prayers from Latin into the language of the people, and had shortened and simplified them. Luther had introduced the singing of hymns. Calvin, like Luther, desired to have the people sing, but instead of hymns he introduced the psalms in meter. That is, Calvin's hymns were like our Old Hundredth, which is made out of the Hundredth Psalm. To Calvin, however, the most important part of the service was the sermon, and the prayers he left for the most part to the discretion of the minister. He paid no heed to the ancient order of service. Thus he established the manner of worship which became common in all the reformed churches, except the Episcopal and Lutheran.

Meanwhile, in Geneva, matters were going from bad to worse. In 1541, Calvin was formally requested to return. He came back the undisputed leader of the Genevan Church. It is characteristic of him that on the first Sunday after his return he took up the course of sermons which had been interrupted by his banishment, and preached as if nothing had happened. He had been preaching on the Epistle to the Romans, and on he went week after week, book by book, and sentence by sentence, through the New Testament and into the Old, during the remaining thirteen years of his life.

Calvin's great purpose was now to make Geneva a City of God.

The first step was to set the Church in order, and this he did on the basis of the New Testament. All the elaborate organizations which had grown through the long centuries of Christian history, he set aside. Finding no bishop in the Bible, he would have none in Geneva. The church officers were pastors, teachers, elders, and deacons, and the elders and deacons were to be laymen. The Church had been governed by the clergy. It had been believed that grace was given them from heaven, and that this grace they gave in turn to the people, through the sacraments. Calvin brought the people themselves into the administration of the Church. The ministers were elected by their fellow-ministers, but they could not enter upon their office until they had the approval of the congregation. These pastors and teachers were called presbyters, and this system by which the presbyters were ordained by other presbyters, was called presbyterian. Thus Calvin, who had changed the old order of worship, by substituting extempore prayer for the prayer-book, changed also the old order of the ministry, by substituting ordination by presbyters for ordination by bishops. He made a complete break with the Ancient Church. He founded, in Geneva, a new Christian society whose only connection with the old was that it held its services in the old churches.

Having thus arranged the Church, the next step was to deal with the lives of the people. This matter the ministers took in hand, and delivered the more serious or obstinate offenders to the magistrates to be punished. All that Calvin had undertaken before was now repeated, and much more. Everybody's private life was under watch and ward. Every house in Geneva was regularly visited, and the inhabitants were questioned as to their knowledge of the Bible and the Catechism, as to their absences from church, and as to any criticism which they might have made in their conversation on the minister. All the family quarrels were examined. All the disobedient children were called to account. If anybody made a noise during a sermon, or laughed in church, or said that the pope was a good man, or that Calvin was a bad man, he was punished. A member of the Little Council, one of the influential men of the city, ventured one time to speak his mind about Calvin, presumably at his own dinner-table. The words were reported, and the rash critic was sentenced to be marched around the streets, dressed in his shirt, bearing a torch in his hand, and to beg the pardon of God and of the government on his knees. A boy who threatened to strike his mother was publicly whipped and banished from the city. A woman who sang an idle song to a psalm tune was beaten with rods. The ministers refused to baptize children with the names of saints, and a small riot arose in the congregation when a child, whose parents wished him to be called "Martin" was named "Abraham" against their will.

Such severities, naturally, angered the people, and in spite of all inspections and punishments, a party of opposition grew in strength. They hindered Calvin; they took the other side in the many controversies in which he was engaged; they named their dogs after him; they put him in peril, not only of his power, but of his life. Then came an enemy named Servetus.

Servetus was a heretic. By profession a physician, and a very skilful one, he was interested also in theology. The Reformation had made it easy to attack all the old beliefs, and of this situation Servetus availed himself. And this he did, not only with much freedom of thought, but with much freedom of expression. It was the fashion of the time for debaters to call one another names, but Servetus carried it to an extreme. Thus he made an assault on the theology of Calvin. He objected to Calvin's ideas both of God and of man. He denied the doctrine of predestination, held that man is able to please God, and rejected the common belief in the Trinity.

In the midst of these discussions, Servetus came in disguise to Geneva, was recognized and arrested in church as he listened to Calvin's preaching, and was put on trial. It was then the general opinion that heresy was an offense to be punished with death; for while a murderer destroyed only the body, a heretic was a poisoner of the soul. Thus Servetus was put in peril of his life. But the case was much more than a single trial for heresy; for all the enemies of Calvin rallied to the defense of the heretic. It was plain that the result of the trial would be the maintaining or the ending of Calvin's power in Geneva.

The man was finally condemned, and sentenced to be burned alive. He sent for Calvin and begged his pardon for any offense which he had committed against him, and asked for an easier death; but this the court would not permit. Thus he died, crying with his last breath, "Jesus, thou Son of the eternal God, have pity on me!"

Calvin continued to be the master of Geneva till the day of his death. He made the city, not only well-behaved, but prosperous. He fostered its trade in silks and velvets; he cleaned its streets. Above all he founded the University of Geneva, a great school of sound learning, whose scholars were afterwards influential all over Europe. The city became a model of what a Christian community should be. Its doctrine, its worship, and its discipline affected all Protestantism, outside of Germany where the ideas of Luther reigned. The Puritans brought the example of Calvin out of England into New England.

In 1903, three hundred and fifty years after the burning of Servetus, a memorial stone was erected on the place of his martyrdom. The first name on the list of subscribers was that of the Consistory of the Genevan Church. This was not a criticism on the act of Calvin, but rather on the age in which he lived. In many respects wiser than his time, he, nevertheless, shared in its errors, even as he breathed its air. That was unavoidable. What to him seemed right, and was the best he knew, to us seems wrong; because the world goes on growing, and grows better.

The theology of Calvin has been in

great part outgrown also. Where he thought of God mainly as the Sovereign of the world, we think of Him rather as the Father of all men. Where he thought of the Bible as a divine book, dictated by God, we think of it as a human book, written by men who increased century by century in the knowledge of God. Where he thought of man as wholly bad, and saved only by the sacrifice of Christ, and even then saved only in part, according to the pleasure of God, without reference to the good or evil of their lives, we think of man as progressing, more and more, towards goodness, by the help of Christ, into an eternal life where everybody shall reap what he has sown.

We see, however, that Calvin's true teaching that God is to be obeyed rather than man, and that in His presence all men, great and small, are valued without regard to wealth or position, made men independent and taught them that the supreme authority is the conscience. It was the foundation of democracy.

And we see also that Calvin's exaltation of the Bible made men study it. There they were to learn the will of God for themselves. There they were to determine what was right and wrong, no matter what was said by Church or state. They must be educated, then, in order to be able to read that book; hence, public schools everywhere, and colleges. Thus for our free and universal education, as well as for our free government, of and by and for the people, we are in debt to Calvin.

As Calvin lay in his last sickness, he summoned the ministers of Geneva to meet him in his room, about his bed, and addressed them as St. Paul addressed the elders of Ephesus. He recounted his labors and his pains, and the hard battles he had fought and won. "What a life it has been," he said, "for a poor scholar, shy and timid as I am." He asked their pardon for his faults, "in particular for his quickness, vehemence, and readiness to be angry." He exhorted them to continue the good work, and taking each one by the hand, he commended them severally to the blessing of God. "We parted from him," says one of them, "with our eyes bathed in tears, and our hearts full of unspeakable grief. " Thus he died, fifty-five years old.

KNOX 1505-1572

John Knox, on the occasion of his first appearance in public, carried a two-handed sword. Up to that moment, he had lived for forty years in obscurity, after that he lived for twenty-five years in public activity.

In 1505, when Knox was born, Henry the Seventh was king of England; Cranmer was a college student in Cambridge; Luther, in that very year, entered the monastery. Calvin was not born till 1509. There Was already much dissatisfaction with the condition of religion, and men were talking about reforms, but there had been no great changes. The world was still in the Middle Ages.

Knox was born at Haddington, due east from Edinburgh, between the hills of Lamias JOHX KXOX

From a Print in the Possession of the New York Public Library mermoor and the Firth of Forth. When the wind blew from the south, it brought the breath of the hills; when it blew from the north, it brought the breath of the sea. The town was small, but it contained three monasteries. It was devoted to the old ways. Whoever looked in any direction in the streets saw a monk or a friar in his gown of black or gray. The principal church was called the "Lamp of Lothian." There was born the man who became the Lamp of Scotland.

Knox's parents were plain people, perhaps farmers. He was always a countryman; he loved the open fields and disliked cities. He spoke of the crowded populations of great towns as the rascal multitude.

Having studied in the schools at home, he went, at the age of seventeen, to the University of Glasgow, where a Haddington man, John Major, was a professor. Thus he became a priest. It was a time when almost all work which demanded intelligence of the scholarly kind was done by priests. Knox was both a lawyer and a schoolmaster. He lived as a tutor, now in this great house and now in that, and taught the children. Thus he continued in peace and quiet till he was forty.

But the Reformation was coming on. Luther nailed his theses to the door, and the sound of his hammer was heard all over Europe. Henry the Eighth destroyed the monasteries. Earnest men in Scotland were considering what to do. And Knox was reading the seventeenth chapter of St. John. This we know because when Knox was in his last illness, and one who stood by read that chapter at his request, "Here," he said, "I first cast anchor." "This is life eternal," it says there, " to know Thee the only true God, and Jesus Christ whom Thou hast sent." The words seemed to clear away all the old complications of religion, and to make the long services and the many priests unnecessary.

Under these conditions, the Reformation blazing in Germany and England, and scattering cinders over Scotland, and the hearts of men beginning to burn within them, the crisis came in two tragedies. One was the martyrdom of George Wishart, who was burned alive at St. Andrews by the order of Cardinal Beaton, for teaching the Greek Testament, and supporting the new opinions. The other was the assassination of Beaton by the friends of Wishart, who burst in upon him, stabbed him in his palace, and seized the cathedral of St. Andrews.

With these tragedies, the obscurity of Knox ended, and his public activity began. For Wishart was Knox's friend. The house in which he was arrested, and from which he was carried to the stake, was the one in which Knox was living as a tutor. As the enemies of the reformer had increased, and it had become plain that he was in peril of death, the tutor had become his body-guard. That was why Knox had the two-handed sword. But Wishart would not let him use it. "One," he said, "is sufficient for a sacrifice."

When the cardinal was killed, Knox joined the garrison at St. Andrews, taking his pupils with him. There he taught the gospel of St. John, not only to his pupils, but to an increasing company. It was plain that he had learning, and eloquence, and courage. Then, one Sunday in the church, the minister, in the midst of his sermon, called on Knox to become a leader and a preacher. The appeal had been planned beforehand, but Knox knew nothing of it. The time was one of excitement and great danger. Everybody in the church knew that before many days the place would be besieged, by an army, to avenge the murder of the cardinal. They had committed the murder; they had done a thing which could not be forgiven. The preacher in the pulpit was afterwards burned at the stake, and the man at whom he pointed his finger and called him to stand up and speak, knew that the summons was like the sending of a soldier into the danger of death.

At first, Knox, in his surprise, rose up and went out and hid himself in his room, and there stayed for some days praying. Then he came back, and went into the pulpit, and preached so that the ears of the hearers tingled. Men said, "Wishart himself never spoke so plainly." They said, "Others snipped the branches; this man strikes at the root."

The twenty-five remaining years of Knox's life fall into two clearly marked and even divisions. During the first part of this time he lived mostly in exile; during the second part, he lived in Scotland.

He went immediately into exile. The Catholics did not sit silent and suffer their cardinal to be killed in peace. They got help from France, and a French fleet besieged St. Andrews, and the garrison had to surrender. The reformers were put into the galleys, and there, in chains, served at the oars, as slaves under the whip. In after years, Knox rarely spoke of this bitter experience. But two incidents are remembered.

One time, he said, a priest who ministered to the prisoners carried about among them the image of a saint for them to kiss, but one of them seized the image and flung it overboard, crying, "Let us see if she can swim: she is light enough!"

Another time, the ship sailed near the coast of Scotland, and there in the distance were the spires of St. Andrews. Knox was very ill, so that they doubted if he would recover, but they pointed out the land, and asked him if he recognized it. "Yes," he said, raising himself on his elbow, "I know it well; for I see the steeple of that place where God first, in public, opened my mouth to His glory; and I am fully persuaded, how weak soever I now appear, that I shall not depart this life till that my tongue shall glorify His godly name in the same place."

Somehow this pain came to an end; probably because of the Protestant supremacy in England under Edward the Sixth. In 1549, the year of the first English Prayer-book, Knox was preaching, by Cranmer's appointment, at Newcastle. Two years later, he was one of the king's six chaplains, and might have been a bishop, if he would. Then Mary came to the throne, the whole state of religion was changed, and Knox, with other reformers, fled to the continent. There he ministered, at first in Frankfort, then in Geneva.

At Frankfort, the refugees were of two parties, moderate and radical. The moderate reformers wished to use the Prayerbook, which represented the English Reformation. The radical reformers, led by Knox, desired to depart from the old order completely. One party was of the mind of Cranmer, the other was of the mind of Calvin. The moderates prevailed, and Knox, after a visit to Scotland, settled in Geneva.

"Geneva," he said, "is the most perfect school of Christ that ever was in the earth since the days of the Apostles. In other places, I confess, Christ is to be truly preached; but manners and religion as truly reformed have I not seen in any other place." There he published a book on predestination, filled with the theology of Calvin. There he published also a book entitled "A First Blast Against the Monstrous Regiment — Government of Women," declaring that it was a horrible thing, contrary to Nature and to the will of God that a woman should sit upon a throne. The particular woman whom he had in mind was Queen Mary, but unhappily for him she was followed by Queen Elizabeth, who so disliked the book that she would never permit the writer to set foot again in England.

Nevertheless, the accession of Elizabeth ended the exile of Knox. He returned to Scotland.

Scotland is a land of picturesque beauty, full of lakes and hills, and moors covered with heather; and it has for its capital one of the most beautiful cities in the world. The land is rich in memories of heroes, sung in ballads; and it has been glorified in the pages of one of the greatest of novelists, Sir Walter Scott. But its history is hard to read. This is mainly for lack of central interest. In the old contention between the barons and the kings, the kings were victorious in England, but the barons were victorious in Scotland. Scotland was, therefore, a land of barons, where a thousand little wars were waged between castle and castle. The history is for the most part like a canvas crowded with small figures. Carlyle said that it contained nothing of world-interest but the reformation by Knox.

The events which followed the return of Knox were of world-interest because, for the moment, the destinies of the whole reforming movement depended on Scotland. On one side were Catholic France and Spain; on the other side were Protestant Germany and England. And the two sides were evenly matched. Scotland, therefore, held the balance. If it declared itself Protestant, the Reformation was saved; if it continued Catholic, the Reformation was endangered, if not lost.

To this situation dramatic interest was added by the appearance on the stage of affairs of the strong, distinct, and contrasted figures, John Knox and Mary Queen of Scots. The whole world looked on at the contention of these two.

Mary was by temperament and training a French woman. She was beautiful in appearance, but her chief charm was in her manner. She had a fascinating influence over all who knew her. She was gay and clever, graceful and accomplished. And she was a Catholic, devoted to the Catholic cause.

Knox was fifty-six years old when

Mary, at the age of nineteen, returned from France to Scotland. He was a sternfaced man, with a long beard. Of the graces and amusements of life he had had no experience. Born on a farm, chained to an oar in a French galley, the neighbor and disciple of Calvin, his ideas of life were totally different from Mary's. He was not disposed to soften or disguise the difference. He had a terrific plainness of speech. And he was devoted, heart and soul, to the Protestant cause.

Knox had the advantage of appearing first upon the scene. He found Scotland in the midst of civil war. Protestants and Catholics were fighting for supremacy. One day, in Edinburgh, after Knox had preached against idolatry, a priest began to say the mass. And a boy threw a stone against the altar. Thereupon the congregation rose up in riot, and having destroyed the images in the church, went out and pulled down three great monasteries. And what was done in Edinburgh was done in other places also. The splendid churches were defaced; the ancient services were stopped. One side called for help from France; the other side called for help from England. The voice of Knox, it was said, was more terrible than the sound of five hundred trumpets.

For a year, between the death of Mary of Lorraine and the coming of Mary Queen of Scots, the throne was empty, and the power was in the hands of a parliament. The parliament adopted a Confession of Faith, which was composed by Knox, and was according to the doctrines of Calvin. They abolished the authority of the pope in Scotland. They forbade attendance at the service of the mass, and declared that anybody who was three times convicted of this offense should be put to death. Thus in the place of the old Catholic intolerance, they introduced a Protestant intolerance.

Meanwhile, the reformers were gathering congregations, sometimes in the parish churches, sometimes outside of them; and now representatives of these societies were summoned to meet in a General Assembly. They adopted a Book of Discipline. It was provided that ministers should be appointed, not by the bishops, but by the people. It was arranged that in Scotland, as in Geneva, everybody's daily conduct should be watched and directed. The ministers were to see to it that the people neither drank too much nor ate too much, that they were honest in their business, and sober in their conversation. If any man refused to obey the minister, nobody was allowed to speak to him, except his wife, his family, and the minister. It was arranged also that the minister and his wife and children should be subject to the judgment of the congregation. Attention was to be paid to the way in which the minister spent his salary: he must neither spend too much nor save too much. The ministers were directed to meet together every week and discuss each other's conduct. Each in turn was to be frankly criticised by his brethren.

The Book of Discipline taught also that out of the tithes or taxes the state should pay, not only preachers, but teachers and relieve the poor. There were to be public schools and universities for the instruction of all the youths of the country, to be paid for out of the lands and other possessions of the Catholic Church. But this the lords and nobles declined to undertake, preferring to keep these lands and treasures for themselves, as had been done in England.

Only one thing was now needed to make Scotland like Geneva. The Confession of Faith had substituted the theology of Calvin for the theology of the past; the Book of Discipline had substituted the New Presbyterianism for the old Episcopacy; and now the Book of Common Order did away with the ancient services, and put preaching and extempore prayer in the place of them.

Thus, when Mary came she found herself the Catholic Queen of a Protestant nation. The rain was falling heavily on the day when she landed in Scotland, the sky was dark, and everything had a dismal and forbidding look. The land seemed very different from France, and she disliked it greatly. Immediately, she found herself in contention with her people.

On the Sunday after her arrival, the mass was said in her chapel at Holyrood. Knox, in his sermon at St. Giles's, declared that one mass was more dangerous to the country than an invading army of ten thousand men. The Queen called the preacher to the palace. "It seems," she said, "to be your purpose to make my subjects obey you rather than me." Knox answered that his purpose was to lead both princes and subjects to obey God. Thus the two first met. "Think ye," said Mary, "that subjects, having power, may resist their princes?" "If their princes exceed their bounds, Madam," answered Knox, "they may be resisted, and even deposed."

The Queen held a ball at Holyrood, in celebration—it was said—of a victory of the Catholics over the Protestants in France. And Knox preached about it. When the Queen called him to account, he told her that she had been misinformed. If she would come to church, he said, she would know what was being preached.

Meanwhile, the young queen was making friends. Some of them liked the pleasures of the court, where there were good things to eat and drink, and plenty of music and dancing. These were young people, to whom Knox and the ministers, with their hard rules and stern questions, and their long prayers and sermons, seemed out of all sympathy with the natural desires of youth. Other friends liked the ancient Church and its rich services, the candles and the singing, the colors and the ceremonies. They felt that it was unjust to forbid them to say their prayers in their own way. They hoped that Mary would succeed till all the new fashions in religion should be abolished, and Knox should be sent back to Geneva.

It is possible that these hopes might have been fulfilled, if Mary had been wise. Already, the mass was being said, in spite of the law, not only at court, but in some of the great houses of the nobility. And it was reported that the queen was about to marry the son of the Catholic king of Spain. It was plain that such a marriage, bringing the power of

Spain to reinforce the Church, would be the end of the authority of Knox. He preached about it, and again the queen called him to the palace.

"What have you to do with my marriage?" she cried. "I have borne with you in all your rigorous manner of speaking, yea, I have sought your favor by all possible means, and yet I cannot be quit of you. I vow to God I shall be revenged."

And she turned upon him, in tears and great anger. "What are you within this realm?"

To which Knox answered, "A subject born within the same."

Thus he declared the right of the people to rule themselves. Because he represented the people, though he was but a farmer's son, he stood on an equality with kings.

Whatever influence the queen had gained, she lost it by her own folly. She married her cousin, Henry Darnley, and within a year showed such favor to a young Italian, Rizzio, that Darnley stabbed him to death in the queen's room. Then she fell in love with the young Earl of Bothwell, and, within a year of the murder of Rizzio, Darnley was killed; the house in which he slept being blown up by gunpowder, exploded—it was believed—by the hands of Bothwell. Three months afterwards, Mary married Bothwell. But this was more than the country could endure. She was seized by the people and compelled to resign her crown. After one decisive battle, in which great numbers of the nobility fought upon her side, she was compelled to flee to England, where she lived for twenty years, till, in the contentions of the time, accused of conspiracy against Elizabeth, she was beheaded.

Great Britain was made Protestant by the action of two queens. The people were slow to change from the old religion to the new. The Reformation was finally established in Scotland, when the people came to hate the Catholic Church because of the follies of Mary Queen of Scots. It was finally established in England, when the people came to hate the Catholics because of the cruelties of Bloody Mary. The two Marys were mainly responsible for it: one of them by marrying Bothwell, the other by burning Cranmer.

Knox preached at the coronation of Mary's infant son, King James. The pulpit of St. Giles resounded with his sturdy sermons. One time when the French ambassador complained to the Town Council that Knox had denounced the king of France, the Council said, "It is very likely. We cannot prevent him from denouncing us." Being driven out of Edinburgh, for a time, by enemies, he went to St. Andrews. One describes how the old man went on preaching-days to the parish church, fur about his neck, a staff in his hand, and his servant, Richard, helping him along. "Then, by the same Richard and another servant, he was lifted up to the pulpit, where he behoved to lean at his first entrance; but, ere he had done with his sermon, he was so active and vigorous that he was like to ding the pulpit in blads and fly out of it." To "ding the pulpit in blads" means to break it in pieces. It is an interesting picture of Knox preaching.

Returning to Edinburgh, he was strong enough to preach a fierce sermon about the Massacre of St. Bartholomew. His last public appearance was at the installation of his successor. Out he went, after the service, leaning on his staff.

Beside the grave of John Knox the Earl of Morton said, "Here lieth a man who in his life never feared the face of man." GASPARD DE COLIGNY

From a Painting by J. A. van Ravesteijn in the Rijksmuseum at Amsterdam COLIGNY

1519-1572

From the windows of his ancient castle, Gaspard de Coligny could look out over miles of mountain and stream and forest, all of which belonged to him.

Coligny seemed to have everything that the heart of man could wish. He was rich and eminent. His family had been great in France for more than four hundred years. Indeed, he traced back his ancestry to the first soldier who followed Clovis into the water of baptism. For Clovis, king of the wild Franks, in the fifth century, made a vow in the midst of a battle that if he won the victory he would become a Christian; and he did win the victory, and was baptized, and three thousand of his warriors with him. The first man to step down into the water after the king, was the forefather of Coligny.

His mother, being left a widow, had given great care to the education of her four sons. They were taught the knightly games of tilt and tourney, in which they played at war, and learned how to give blows and take them. They were trained in the courteous manners of the time. They could sing the ballads which celebrated the courage of the heroes of Charlemagne, and could read them in the pages of the books. Also they could read the New Testament, which had just been translated into French. One of the boys was made a cardinal, at the age of sixteen; one died; the other two, Gaspard and Andelot, were brought to the court of King Francis the First.

Here was a gay life of balls and tournaments, with an occasional experience of real fighting, in the wars which were always going on. Here Coligny met young Francis of Lorraine, known later as the Duke of Guise, and the two became fast friends, jousting in the same tournaments, dancing at the same parties, wearing the same colors, white and green, and each planning to become the greatest captain of his age. Already the two friends showed the qualities which afterwards made them enemies. Guise desired to have his pleasure; Coligny to do his duty. Guise was an aristocrat, caring only for persons of high birth and wealth; Coligny cared for the common people.

So years passed, and Francis died and Henry the Second came to the throne, with Catherine de' Medici his wife. Henry and Catherine, Guise and Coligny, were all young together. It was Guise who held the town of Metz against the tremendous forces of Charles the Fifth. It was Coligny who brought order and discipline into the army of France.

The soldiers who fought for France came from various countries for the sake of the French pay. They were wild and lawless, and their only interest was to get whatever spoil they could. When war was in progress they fought the enemy, but in the intervals of peace they fought among themselves. They were as uncontrolled as savage animals. These soldiers Coligny brought under stern rule. He hated disorder. He hated still more the oppression of the weak at the hands of the strong. Every robber, he promptly hanged. Men who committed lesser offenses were beaten with the hafts of pikes. Even swearing was punished with the pillory. Thus the general saved the people from the soldiers, and introduced into the army a drill, a discipline, a life under severe rule, such as is common enough now, but which had not then been known since the time of the old Caesars.

At the age of thirty-three, Coligny was made Admiral of France. But the fortunes of war now turned against him. At the siege of St. Quentin, he was taken prisoner by the Spaniards. During the quiet months of his imprisonment, while he waited for the ransom by which he was released, he had opportunity to think, not only about war, but about religion. He became a Huguenot.

The Huguenots were the Protestants of France. The name indicates their position as a people already persecuted. One of the gates of the city of Tours was named for old King Hugo, about whom there were many pleasant ghost-stories. The king was said to be in the habit of coming out of his grave by night, and wandering about the streets. The Protestants of the city, being in fear of their neighbors, used to meet at King Hugo's gate, under the cover of darkness. They were called Huguenots in derision, because like the ghostly king they appeared only at night.

Protestantism had come into France gradually, assisted by many influences: by the lives of the clergy, which suggested the common phrase, " as idle as a priest"; by the desire of the monks for money; by the enlightenment of the new learning; by the sermons of Luther, and by the satires of Rabelais; by the teaching of Calvin. Little by little, the new opinions made their way. First in this town, then in that, those who thus agreed in the necessity of changing religion for the better came together and founded Protestant societies.

These people had no leader. No Luther, no Cranmer, no Calvin had appeared in France. But they had their heroes. One of their first martyrs was a poor wool-carder of Meaux, named Leclerc. A papal bull had been posted on the cathedral door, promising the usual indulgences to those who should repeat certain prayers. Leclerc tore it down. He was three times publicly whipped for this offense and his forehead was branded with the fleur-de-lis. In spite of these punishments, hearing that a procession was starting to go to a saint's shrine outside the city, he hurried out before the people and destroyed the shrine. When the procession arrived, they found the image of the saint in pieces. For this, they cut off Leclerc's right hand, tore his face and breast with pincers, and finally put upon his head a red-hot band of iron. He made no groan nor cry, but continued, so long as he had breath, to recite the text, "Their idols-are silver and gold, the work of men's hands." And there were many like him; but most of them were plain people. The nobles, the bishops, the scholars held, for the most part, to the old ways.

When Henry the Second became king he entered upon a vigorous course of persecution, treating the Huguenots as if they were poisonous weeds in a garden. But this seemed only to increase their number. Every martyr converted a hundred indifferent or hostile persons into disciples. Torture had no terror for them. Men, women, and children marched to their punishment as if they were on their way to a merry festival, singing as they went. As they died, they turned their faces toward Geneva, blessing God for John Calvin.

For the Huguenots were Calvinists. They liked the methods of Calvin better than the methods of Cranmer.

There are two ways of dealing with a tree which has ceased to bear good fruit. One way is to take a pruning-knife, and lop off some of the dead branches, and a grafting-knife, and set new branches in their place. That is what Cranmer did. He kept the old service, only making it more simple and translating it into English. He kept the old Church, only subtracting the pope, who, after all, had been added to the apostolic order in the Middle Ages.

The other way is to take an ax. The tree bears no good fruit: cut it down, and plant another. That is what Calvin did. He put away the book which contained the old prayers, and told the ministers to make new prayers for themselves, out of their own hearts. He put away the bishops, and told the ministers that they were each as good as any bishop. Thus he established new societies of Christians; in France, called Huguenots; in Scotland, called Presbyterians.

In his prison, Coligny became a Huguenot. He brought to the service of these people the might of his own personality, and the strength of his high position. When the war was over, and the Admiral's ransom was paid, and he was free, he found himself at the head of the Protestant party in France; the papal party was led by his old companion, the Duke of Guise.

Between these parties was the Queenmother, Catherine de' Medici. She was the ruler of France. After the death of her husband, Henry the Second, her sons came to the throne: first Francis the Second, at the age of sixteen; and after his death, Charles the Ninth, at the age of ten. The real power was in her hands.

At a meeting of the Assembly of Notables to consider the condition of the kingdom, Coligny presented a petition, "the supplication of those who, in divers provinces, invoke the name of God, according to the rule of piety." It was a request that the Huguenots might be permitted to practise their religion without hindrance.

"But," cried Guise, "the petition is unsigned."

"I will get fifty thousand signatures in Normandy alone," said Coligny.

"And I," said Guise, "will get five hundred thousand who will oppose it with their blood."

It was finally agreed to call a national

parliament to discuss the matter, and after some years, and many obstructions put by the Guises in the way, such an assemblage was gathered together. An edict was passed giving the Protestants the right to meet, under the protection of the law. And there were those who hoped, that in France as in England, the men of the old learning and the men of the new, might somehow get along in peace.

But one day, six weeks after the issuing of the edict, the Duke of Guise, with an escort of gentlemen and soldiers, was riding on his way to Paris. And they came on a Sunday morning to the little town of Vassy. And the Huguenots of Vassy, in the freedom which the law had given them, were holding a religious service in a large barn.

"What is this?" said the Duke of Guise.

"It is a Huguenot meeting," said somebody who stood by.

"I will Huguenot them," cried the Duke. And thereupon he marched his soldiers against the barn; they broke the doors, and fired upon the people, men, women, and children, all unarmed and defenseless, till more than sixty of them were killed, and two hundred were wounded.

This was the beginning of a series of wars of religion which lasted for ten years. The men of the old religion were strong in the cities; the strength of the men of the new religion was in the villages. Neighbors fought against neighbors. Soon, two armies were in the field, and there were bloody battles, sometimes with success on one side, sometimes with success on the other. Guise was the leader of the Catholics, Coligny of the Protestants. The forces seemed to be evenly matched. The whole land was in distress.

Then, one day, a young Huguenot soldier and spy, pretending to be a Catholic, got admission to the household of the Duke of Guise and shot him, and then said that he had been sent to do that deed by Admiral Coligny. The Admiral denied it. He confessed that he was glad that the Duke was dead, for he believed him to be an enemy of God, but he declared that he had no part in killing him. They who have examined the matter most carefully find him innocent. But the tragedy added bitterness to a situation which was already bitter enough.

So campaign followed campaign across the fair land of France, each leaving a trail of burned houses and desecrated churches and dead bodies. Coligny's brother Andelot, after valiant service in the Huguenot armies, died of fever. Coligny's splendid castle was sacked, and his books, his pictures, all his treasures were destroyed. His fortune was gone. He had given to the cause of religion all that he had. When the news came of the plunder of his castle he wrote to his boys, "We must not count upon what is called property, but rather place our hope elsewhere than on earth." Suddenly, with an army which increased like a rolling snowball, he marched on Paris. And Catherine, in great fear, made terms of peace. She granted what Coligny had been fighting for, liberty in religion.

So there was peace in France, but only on the surface. The land was filled with rumors of disorder. At any moment, the old enemies might fall to fighting. It seemed to Coligny that there was only one way to unite the people of France, and to secure the lasting safety of the Huguenots. That was to go to war with Spain. Spain was the ancient foe of France, and was occupied just then in putting down a Protestant revolution in the Netherlands. Coligny proposed that the armies of France should direct their energies towards the Netherlands. Thus should Spain be humbled; the Netherlands would be added to the domains of France; and the cause of Protestantism would be greatly strengthened in Europe. This he said, day by day, to the young king. And in this he was day by day opposed by Catherine de' Medici, the king's mother. She was against the war; and especially she was against sending French forces to help the Dutch Protestants resist the Spanish Catholics.

In the midst of these discussions, all the nobility of France came crowding into Paris to attend a wedding. Margaret of Valois was to be married to Henry of Navarre. Henry was a Protestant, Margaret was a Catholic, and the union of the two seemed to represent the peace of the divided nation. The heart of Coligny was filled with hope. As he walked in the church of Notre Dame, after the wedding was over, he waved his hand toward the flags which hung upon the walls, memorials of Huguenot defeats, and said to a companion, "Soon shall these be pulled down, and better flags put in their places." It was plain, however, to observant persons, that Coligny was in danger. He was warned again and again to leave Paris. There were cautious friends who begged him to escape while he could from a city wherein Catherine was the ruler, and the young Duke of Guise had succeeded to his father's place. But Coligny trusted the king.

At last, one day, when the wedding festivities, the banquets, and the masquerades were over, Coligny met the king on his way to play a game of tennis, and went with him and looked on. As he started to go home, a man handed him a petition and he walked slowly along the street, reading as he went. Suddenly came the report of a gun, and Coligny felt himself struck by bullets in his right hand and his left arm. It was evident that an assassin had tried to kill him. The house was searched, from whose window the gun was fired, but nobody was found. Coligny was carried to his lodgings, and a physician was summoned. The king came to visit the wounded man, and so did Catherine. The people suspected the Duke of Guise. There were threatening cries against him in the streets.

The visit of sympathy was followed by a hasty meeting of the Council. What should be done? The Huguenots were demanding that the murderer be found and punished, and were declaring openly that the real murderer was Guise himself. The civil war seemed likely to begin again. Again there would be armies in the bloody fields, and Frenchmen would be killing Frenchmen. Again the Protestants would be led against the Catholics. It seemed to Catherine that for the sake of the nation and for the sake of the Catholic religion, there was only one thing to be done. That was to put to death not Coligny only, but all the Huguenot leaders then in Paris. Such an operation of surgery, she thought, might save France. "The dead do not make war."

So a massacre was planned. The young king, who was more than half disposed to take the counsels of Coligny, and had listened to him with regard and affection, was reluctantly persuaded. The Catholics were to wear a white handkerchief around the left arm. The Duke of Guise was to have the responsibility of murdering the Admiral. The houses of the Huguenots were marked. Even then the victims did not suspect the intentions of their enemies. So midnight passed, and the hands of the clock pointed to three or four of the morning of August 24, the feast of St. Bartholomew. Then the king, urged by his mother, gave the order to ring the bell of the church of St. Germain.

Immediately, the attack began. The house of Coligny was assaulted, and an entrance made. The wounded man was lifted up by his servants, while the noise of the enemy increased. A Huguenot minister prayed beside him. Coligny commended his soul in faith to God. Then they broke in, and killed him, and threw his body out of the window into the courtyard, where the Duke of Guise was waiting.

Then, for three days, blood ran in the gutters of Paris. Under the protection of the court, and with the aid of soldiers, the Catholics hunted the Protestants in the streets. Almost all of the Huguenot leaders were killed; and of the people, nobody knows how many: two thousand, six thousand, eight thousand, in Paris; and in the country, ten to twenty thousand.

When the news reached Rome, the city was illuminated during the nights of the greater part of a week, the guns of the Castle of St. Angelo were fired, the pope, with all the ambassadors and cardinals in their robes, marched in procession to the church, where a mass of thanksgiving was celebrated. The choir sang the twentyfirst psalm: "The king shall rejoice in thy strength, O Lord; exceeding glad shall he be of thy salvation. Thou hast given him his heart's desire, and hast not denied him the request of his lips. All thine enemies shall feel thine hand: thy right hand shall find out them that hate thee." Every word seemed appropriate. A papal medal was struck to commemorate the massacre.

This rejoicing of Christian men over the bodies of their enemies seems almost as horrible as the massacre itself. Other Christians, Catholic as well as Protestant, denounced it. One of the last thundering sermons of John Knox was preached against it. To the pope, however, the news came like the tidings of victory in battle. He overlooked the black treachery of it in honest gratitude that the enemies of the Church were fallen.

Thus Coligny died a martyr, and the cause to which he gave his noble life died with him. For a time, the Huguenots were tolerated in their weakness. Finally, by the Revocation of the Edict of Nantes, they were driven out of France.

The Reformation failed in France for many reasons, but chiefly because the people did not want it. When the Reformation was over in Europe, and all the battles had been fought and all the armies were disbanded, and the smoke had blown away enough to make it possible to see the resulting situation, it was found that the line between the countries in which the new religion failed and in which it succeeded ran along national and racial boundaries. On one side were the people who spoke German, and languages like German, such as Dutch and English. On the other side were the people who spoke languages which were derived from Latin, such as French, Spanish, and Italian. The inference is that the Reformation naturally attracted those who cared greatly for freedom, and repelled those who cared greatly for order. It was in accordance with the idea of the liberty of the individual; it was not in accordance with the idea of the authority of the institution. Anyhow, the northern nations received it, and the southern nations refused it.

As for Coligny, his cause failed; but courage and devotion never fail. The men who do battle for the sake of truth and right may be defeated, but their memory becomes a priceless possession. The example of a man who gives up ease, and wealth, and the pleasures of comfortable success, and life itself for a good cause, is an inspiring influence to all time. Coligny's name is a great victory. Men have ever since been braver and better because of him.

WILLIAM THE SILENT 1533-1584

Charles The Fifth, King of Spain, Emperor of Germany, "Absolute Dominator" of Asia, Africa, and America, and (incidentally) hereditary sovereign of the seventeen provinces of the Netherlands, retired from his exalted position and gave his lands and his power to his son Philip.

At the dramatic ceremony, in the Hall of the Golden Fleece at Brussels, the emperor's son stood at his right hand. Philip was twenty-eight years old; a small, slender, sickly man, with light hair, and beard thin and pointed, his lower lip protruding like the lips of all the Hapsburgs, his chest contracted, his legs spindling and unsteady.

By the emperor's left hand stood his favorite subject, upon whose shoulders the 168 WILLIAM THE SILENT

From a Painting by Frans Floris (de Vriendt) in the Gallery at Kassel infirm sovereign leaned as he read his valedictory address. William of Orange, scion of a family so distinguished that his ancestors, as he once proudly said, had occupied illustrious positions while the Hapsburgs were obscure squires in Switzerland, had become, at fifteen, a page in the imperial court, had risen, at eighteen, to be one of the emperor's trusted counselors, at twenty-one had commanded an army, and was now the chief citizen of the Netherlands. He was six years the junior of Philip, but was taller and better looking; erect and alert, his hair and beard dark as Philip's were light, he was the embodiment of grace and dignity and strength. Thus they stood, on either side of the king, who were thenceforth to be the bitterest of enemies, and to fight each other in one of the fiercest of wars.

The two men differed, not only in appearance, but in principle. They stood for antagonistic ideas both in politics and in religion.

There are two theories in politics as to the proper residence of power. According to one theory, power should be centralized; it should be in the hands of officers whose business is to rule the people; as for the people, their duty is to do as they are told and to think as they are taught. According to the other theory, power should be distributed; it should be in the hands of officers who are the servants, not the masters, of the people; and all alike, whether sovereigns or subjects, should obey the laws which the people themselves make.

These two theories came into conflict when the barbarians invaded the Roman Empire. The first had been held by the Latins and their neighbors south of the Rhine; the second by the Germans and their neighbors north of the Rhine. But the conquering nations of the north accepted in great part the political ideas of the conquered nations of the south. In the sixteenth century, the theory that power ought to be centralized was practically universal in Europe. The imposing titles of Charles the Fifth represented it. At the same time, the ancient spirit of liberty was beginning to assert itself. Thus the Reformation was, everywhere, not only a religious but a political movement. The local state and the local Church together declared their independence. In Germany the electors, each of whom ruled a community of citizens and resented the dictation of the emperor, protected Luther, who was encouraging communities of Christians to reject the authority of the pope. And in England the independence of the Church was a part of the independence of the nation. In Switzerland, where the state was weak, Calvin was able to make the Church free from all political control. In France, where the state was strong, Coligny tried in vain to give the people the right to choose their own religion without regard to the religion of the king. In the Netherlands, Philip stood for centralization, demanding that the people should obey him and the pope. William stood for national and religious independence.

The religious ideas which the two men represented were equally opposed. On one side was the principle of uniformity, on the other side the principle of liberty. The theory of Philip was that all men should behave and believe alike. They should have the same church, the same service, and the same creed. That was also the theory of Henry the Eighth, who desired, indeed, that England should be independent, but who insisted that, in England, there should be but one custom and one faith. It was the theory of Calvin, who wished to expel from Geneva all who disagreed with him. It was the general principle of the time, and was held, not only by bigots and fanatics, but by almost all good men.

On the other side was the principle of liberty. This was the idea that not only nations but individuals had the right to differ. According to this theory a man might be a Catholic or a Protestant as he preferred, following his own conscience; and in the same nation, Catholics and Protestants might live together, each going his own way, and neither persecuting his neighbor. This was the conviction of William. It is plain enough now, and prevails everywhere. But at that time, it prevailed nowhere. It was made a part of our life by the success of the long war which William fought against Philip.

Philip and William represented, not only the difference between the ideas of centralization and of representation in politics, and between the ideas of uniformity and of liberty in religion, but between Spain and Holland. In Holland, prominence was given to the people; in Spain, the prominent powers were priests and princes.

The Dutch were the most industrious people in Europe. They were, accordingly, more wealthy than their neighbors, and their wealth, having been earned by their own labors, was expended for the general good. The architects of other countries erected castles and cathedrals; they were in the employ of the princes and the priests. In the Netherlands also there were castles and cathedrals, but architecture did not stop there. Town halls, guild houses, and palaces of private citizens adorned the Dutch cities. In England, the vast walls of the cathedral of Durham looked from their green hill upon a village of mean houses, where the smoke of the hearth rose through holes in the roof, while the bell-tower of the cathedral of Antwerp stood amidst five hundred mansions of marble.

The artists of Italy and Spain painted for the court, the cloister, and the Church. Their scenes were laid in heaven, or in those dimly imagined Bible lands which seemed almost as remote; and their subjects were the symbols of theology,—the Madonna and Child, the crucifixion, the resurrection, repeated over and over,—or the supernatural adventures of the saints. But the artists of the Netherlands painted for the people also, making pictures which were meant to be hung in parlors and dining-rooms. They described the life which they saw about them, trees and flowers and running water, birds and babies, the men and women of the neighborhood in their everyday dress. Presently, the desire of the people to have pictures, even when they had but humble walls on which to hang them, led to the art of engraving; and that led to printing.

The printing-press in the Netherlands was used for the benefit of the people. The Dutch, in the sixteenth century, were the best educated nation in Europe. Art, poetry, and philosophy were at their height in Italy; but common education, the instruction of the people, flourished in the Low Countries as nowhere else. They had their public schools, supported by the state, for the training of young citizens. At a time when noblemen in other countries made their mark because they did not know how to write their names, every child in Holland owned a primer, and there were many cities in which most of the children of the age of ten could write and speak two languages. Every town had its literary society, its guild of rhetoric.

The government of the country was

in keeping with this democratic spirit. The political unit was the trade-union or guild. Representatives of the guilds ruled the towns. Each town sent delegates to the legislature, where they sat with the nobles under the presidency of the stadtholder, who stood for the king. But on important matters all the nobles together had but one vote, while the towns had one apiece, and the power of the stadtholder was limited by written constitutions which secured the liberty of the people.

Into this country, the most industrious, the richest, the best educated, and the most democratic in Europe, came the Reformation. At once, it became a popular movement. In Germany, in France, in England, princes had joined the reformers for their own advantage; but in the Netherlands, it was the people themselves who welcomed the reforms. They had been reading the Bible. There were as many copies of the translated Scriptures in the Dutch provinces as in all the rest of Europe. These Bible-reading people were intelligently appreciative of the new preaching. Roman inquisitors, thinking to stamp the Reformation out, were confronted, not by the princes only, but by the greater part of the population. Before the Duke of Alva began his invasion of the country, more Dutchmen had died for their religion than in all the rest of Europe during all the persecutions of the times. Add together the victims of Bloody Mary in England, of inquisitors in Spain, and of Catherine de' Medici in France, and the sum is small compared with the hundred thousand whose blood and ashes fertilized the soil of the Netherlands. And when the inquisitors were busiest, the people, in great crowds, flocked out into the open fields beside the city gates to listen to the sermons of their preachers, and to show, as they said, how many the inquisitors would have to hang or burn.

Over against these countrymen of William stood the subjects of Philip. Spain was despotic in its government and military in its ambition. There had been a time when the Spaniards had engaged in the occupations of peace. Furnaces and machine-shops, markets and schools, had flourished amongst them. There had been Spanish universities good enough to attract students from other countries. The people had enjoyed a fair degree of freedom.

Then came the year of Spain's two fatal successes: Granada fell, and America was discovered.

Granada fell, and the Moors were expelled from Spain,—the most industrious, intelligent, law-abiding, and prosperous of its inhabitants. The purpose was to make Spain the most Christian of all nations: not a Mohammedan, not a Jew, was to be allowed to live there. Having cleared the land of Jews and Mohammedans, the next step was to clear it of heretics. The Inquisition, which had been intended for the discovery and punishment of Moors, was now turned against Christians who were suspected of sympathy with the reformers. It was a combination of questions and tortures. All the possibilities of pain were used to compel prisoners to confess, and when they confessed they were burned at the stake. This cruelty poisoned the lives of all who took part in it. It changed Spanish religion into bigotry.

Then America was discovered, a land of gold and precious stones, where a handful of adventurers could overcome an ancient nation and make a thousand fortunes. Men abandoned their mills, their merchandise, and their farms. Trade was no longer respectable. The Spaniards turned from their schoolbooks to their swords. No citizen of Spain was ever the source of so much harm to his country as Christopher Columbus. His discovery changed the Spanish character.

Spain and Holland were thus as far apart as they could be. Yet Holland was a member of Spain's household. Philip, on the day of his father's abdication, was put in possession of the Dutch provinces, and William was to be his faithful servant and obey his orders. It was an impossible situation. Between these two men and these two nations, war was inevitable.

The situation was first made plain to William by a memorable talk which he had in a French forest, during a stag hunt, with the king of France. Henry of France and Philip of Spain had been raging a fruitless war between their kingdoms, and had come to terms of peace. William represented Philip in the making of the treaty. Henry, supposing that William was in Philip's confidence in all things, spoke to him about the agreement which the two kings had made to rid their lands of heretics. Henry said that the heretics were increasing in France, and that great men, like Coligny, were on their side, but that he intended to clear the country of the "accursed vermin." He told William how glad he was that Philip had the same intention concerning the Netherlands.

This was all news to William, but he listened without comment. "I confess," he said afterwards, "that I was deeply moved with pity for all the worthy people who were thus devoted to slaughter, and for the country, to which I owed so much, wherein they designed to introduce an inquisition worse and more cruel than that of Spain. From that hour," he said, "I resolved, with my whole soul, to do my best to drive this Spanish vermin from the land." But he said nothing. It was his self-control on this occasion which gave him his name of William the Silent.

William returned straight from this interview to Holland and began the Dutch Revolution. He persuaded the Dutch Parliament, the States-General, to vote no money to the king of Spain till all the

Spanish troops were withdrawn from the country. And this was accomplished. Philip, being thus resisted, though not yet understanding how serious the situation was, went back to Spain. As he stood on the pier, ready to embark, he complained to William concerning the treatment which he had received. "It is the States," said William. "No, no!" cried Philip. "It is you, you, you!"

The main purpose of William at the beginning of the struggle was to protect the Netherlands against a persecution for religion. He was himself a Catholic, though his wife was a Lutheran. It was his desire that the new religion and the old should dwell together in the nation as peacefully as they dwelt under his own roof. "He held it to be cruelty to kill any man simply for maintaining an erroneous opinion. He used to say that in all matters of religion, punishment should be reserved to God alone, much as the rude German who said to the emperor, 'Sire, your concern is with the bodies of your people, not with their souls.'" When the king determined to set up the Inquisition in the Netherlands, William sent him word that he would resist him. "As for myself," he said, " I shall continue to hold by the Catholic faith; but I will never give any color to the tyrannical claim of kings to dictate to the consciences of their people."

Then, one day in Antwerp, there was a religious procession through the streets, and a jeering mob followed it, and fighting began, and the churches were attacked, and before the disorder could be stopped all the images of Antwerp had been broken, and all the stained-glass shattered in the windows. When Philip heard of it, his anger was so great that it made him sick of a fever. "By the soul of my father," he cried, "it shall cost them dear!"

The army which Philip sent against the Netherlands was commanded by the Duke of Alva. He was the foremost soldier in Spain. He had been a man of war from his youth. When he was but four years old, his father was killed by the Moors, and his grandfather taught him to hate heretics. He fought with distinction in an important battle at the age of sixteen. He was now nearly sixty,— tall, thin, erect, with yellow skin and bristling black hair, and a beard long and sable-silvered. He believed that he was fighting in a righteous cause, for the good of the country and the Church.

Alva's errand was to punish those who had been concerned in the disorders at Antwerp and elsewhere. For this purpose he established a Council of Troubles, which was soon called by the people the Council of Blood. Thousands of men and women, guilty and innocent, were put to death. They were hanged on scaffolds, on trees, at the door-posts of private houses. Many of them were poor; but some were the chief citizens and nobles of the country. The whole business of the land was stopped; grass grew in the markets. Every family was in mourning. And against these cruelties the people could do nothing. They had had no experience in war. They were shopkeepers and schoolmasters. The Spanish soldiers had them at their mercy, and they showed no mercy.

Meanwhile, William was trying to hire an army. He was spending his fortune, even to the pledging of his plate and jewels, to assemble soldiers. But when they were assembled Alva and his Spaniards cut them to pieces. William's son, a student in the University of Louvain, was seized and carried off to Spain. William's wife went crazy. Philip pronounced him an outlaw, under the ban of the empire. His neighbors begged him to put down his arms. "Our friends and allies have all turned cold," he said. Yet, "we must have patience and not lose heart, submitting to the will of God, and striving incessantly, as I have resolved to do, come what may. With God's help, I am determined to push onward."

William gathered another army. The soldiers came from Germany, and there were to be reinforcements from France: Coligny was managing that. Then came the tragedy of St. Bartholomew, and the German army was defeated. And the defeat was followed by the massacre of cities. At last, the Dutch began to fight with their own hands. They began to defend their besieged cities. The Spanish soldiers declared that the towns were garrisoned with devils. The women fought, and the children. Battles were waged in the water, and on the ice, and in tunnels under the earth.

Finding that there was no hope of help from France or Germany or England, the Dutch made an alliance with the ocean. Holland lay below the level of the sea, which was kept back by great banks of earth called dikes. When Leyden was besieged, and Spanish camps surrounded the city so that no food could be brought in, and plague and famine were within the walls, William cut the dikes. In came the ocean upon the land, and with it came the relieving ships, floating for six miles over the farms. The besiegers were drowned out, and the city was saved.

The war lasted forty years, till the treaty of peace in 1609. William did not see the end of it. He had been in constant peril of assassins. Again and again, men had been hired by Philip to kill him. Once he was saved by the barking of his little dog. Once he was shot in the face, but not fatally. At last, a man named Gerard Balthazar pretended to be a Protestant, begged money from William to relieve his poverty, bought two pistols with the money, hid himself in William's house at Delft, and murdered him one day as he came out from dinner. This he did, believing that he was doing God service.

But the victory of Holland was the work of William. He had established the independence of his country. He had done even more than that, for he had secured in Holland the supremacy of a new idea. He had not only made the land independent, but he had made it the home of religious liberty. Becoming himself a Calvinist, he protected the Roman Catholics against whom he had fought. He protected the Lutherans and the Baptists, whom the Calvinists hated. He made Holland a place of refuge for all persecuted people. In Amsterdam there were pictures painted on the walls of houses showing a dove escaping from an eagle. The dove represented a Lutheran, a Baptist, a Huguenot, a Puritan, seeking refuge in the only land on earth where men were free to follow their own religion in peace.

When the men who afterwards founded New England were driven out of their own country, they fled to Holland, where they learned lessons which they afterwards put in practice in their colony at Plymouth. The idea of the separation of Church and state, the principle of the freedom of conscience, and the right of honest men to differ in religion, came into this land from the example of William the Silent.

BREWSTER 15 60-1644 UNDER the pillow of William Brewster were the great keys of the city of Flushing. The Dutch were still in the midst of their long war with Spain, and were borrowing men and money from England for reinforcements; and Queen Elizabeth, to make sure of the repayment of the debt, had required that certain Dutch towns should be given over to English garrisons.

Thus, among other places of importance, Flushing was surrendered. The English troops marched to the parish church and said their prayers, and promised, on their solemn oath, to be faithful to their trust, and then proceeded to the fortifications of the town, from which the Dutch quietly retreated. The keys were formally presented to the queen's ambassador, Mr. Davison, and he gave them for safe keeping to his secretary, young Mr. Brewster, who, when he went to bed that night, put them under his pillow.

Brewster, in the due course of events, transferred the keys to the hands of Sir Philip Sidney. Thus, for a moment, we see these two brave men together: Sidney, who said, "When you hear of a good war, go to it," and who, as he lay dying on the field of battle, gave to a private soldier the cup of water which was brought to him; and Brewster, the leader of the Plymouth colonists.

He was far enough, at that time, from any thoughts of leading a company of colonists. He had entered with excellent prospects into the service of the English court. His master, the ambassador, who gave him the keys to keep, presently put about his neck a gold chain with which the Dutch had honored him, telling him to wear it till they returned to London.

It seemed the symbol of a pleasant and distinguished future. Mr. Davison became one of Her Majesty's principal Secretaries of State, and Brewster continued to be a member of his household. Here "the Secretary found him so discreet and faithful that he trusted him above all others that were about him," and esteemed him " rather as a son than as a servant."

Then came the peril of the Armada, and though the winds and storms destroyed the Spanish fleet, there was left in the English mind a nervous terror as to what might happen next. The imagination of the people was filled with the idea of plots against the Queen, and constant rumor suspected Mary Queen of Scots. Thus she was beheaded. In this tragic matter, Secretary Davison bore an official, though unwilling part. He it was, attended perhaps by Brewster, who carried to Elizabeth the warrant for Mary's execution, and who took the paper with the queen's signature to the chancellor. But when the deed was done, and Mary was actually put to death, Elizabeth was overwhelmed with remorse and anger, and these emotions she visited upon her innocent secretary. Davison was sent to the Tower; his honorable career was abruptly ended, and Brewster was without occupation.

Out of the shipwreck of his plans, the young courtier secured an appointment as postmaster of Scrooby. Scrooby was a village in Nottinghamshire. A traveler who passed that way about that time noticed two buildings in the town: "the parish church, not big, but very well builded of square polished stone," and "a great manor place, standing within a moat, and belonging to the Archbishop of York, builded in two courts." In this manor, Brewster resided, "in good esteem among his friends and the good gentlemen of those parts," for nearly thirty years. It was his business, as postmaster, to attend not only to the forwarding of private letters, but to receiving and sending of despatches from the court. There he was married, and there his five children came to gladden his life.

Whatever interest William Brewster may have already taken in religion, he now entered into it with great earnestness. "He did much good in the country where he lived in promoting and furthering religion, not only by his practice and example, and provoking and encouraging others, but by procuring good preachers to the places thereabout, and drawing on of others to assist and help forward in such a work."

The preachers whom Brewster thus brought to minister to Scrooby and the neighborhood lamented the evils of the times. Elizabeth had now been followed by King James, and the wise plans under which the Church of England had been governed were unhappily changed. James brought from Scotland a dislike for Presbyterians which amounted to hatred. He remembered how they had driven his mother, Queen Mary, from her throne, and how they had plagued his youth. He detested the very name of John Knox. He believed that all Presbyterians were the enemies of kings. And he found great numbers of them in England. The men who had come back from exile on the Continent had learned there both the new doctrines and the new customs of Calvin, and they liked them. And people in England liked them. There was a strong desire to make the Church of England as simple as the Church of Geneva. In Geneva there were no bishops, no prayerbooks, no surplices, nothing which had been added to the Christian religion since the New Testament. Why should these things be in England?

The people who were of this opinion were called Puritans. They were still members of the Church of England, and they still hoped that the simplicity which they liked might be had within the church. The ministers who were of this way of thinking desired to be free to wear their own coats instead of the surplice, and to pray their own prayers without reading them out of the book. This freedom they respectfully requested from King James.

The king refused them. "I will none of that," he said. "I will have one doctrine and one discipline, one religion in substance and in ceremony"; and he added, "Either let them conform themselves, and that shortly, or they shall hear of it."

But they did not conform themselves, for they were convinced that they were right. And they heard of it. The ministers who followed the new ways were threatened, and silenced and deprived of their churches, and the people who agreed with them were fined and imprisoned. The result was that the number of Puritans continually increased, and that the Puritans departed further and further from the customs of the Church. Some of them were conservative persons, who felt that Calvin and Knox had gone far enough; these were called Presbyterians. Others, having begun to free themselves from the traditions, went on into larger liberties. They maintained that their minister should be appointed and ordained not by the bishop, and not by any assembly of presbyters, but by themselves, by the people of the congregation. These men were called Independents, or Congregationalists.

The Churchmen of Brewster's neighborhood were Congregationalists. They left the parish church, and met in Brewster's house, where "with great love he entertained them." And they resolved, as fines and imprisonments and other troubles increased, to leave England and go into that country where William the Silent had established freedom in religion. They turned their faces towards Holland.

They chartered a ship to sail from Boston, in Lincolnshire. But even this privilege was denied them. They were forbidden to leave the country. Nevertheless, they made the attempt. At night, they met on board, only to be betrayed by the captain to the police. They were arrested and brought back to land, robbed of their money and their books, and for a time thrust into prison.

The next spring they tried again. They hired a Dutch ship, and began to embark, putting out from the shore in boats. A part of the company were on board, another part, with many of the women and children, were still on the land, when a band of soldiers appeared in the distance in pursuit. The captain hoisted sail, and off he went, the men protesting in vain, their wives and little ones left behind. At last, after a fearful storm, they arrived in Holland. Those who were left were seized by the soldiers and imprisoned; but the injustice of the situation was plain. They had committed no offense; the cost of keeping them in prison seemed a needless burden on the state; they had no homes to which they could be sent back. Finally, they were permitted to make their way, as best they could, to the haven where they would be.

Thus the Scrooby congregation were reunited in Amsterdam in 1608. From Amsterdam, they moved to Leyden: "a beautiful city," they said, "of a sweet situation." Thus Brewster returned to the country which he had visited as a courtier in his youth. The pilgrims were poor, and homesick, and unacquainted with the language of their neighbors, but they had a good courage. They were free at last to worship God in their own way. They made John Robinson their pastor, and chose Brewster to be their ruling elder.

Elder Brewster supported himself by teaching English, and presently by printing books which it was not safe to print in England, mostly concerning the freedom of thought and speech for which he and his companions stood. The matter came even to the notice of King James, and he told the English ambassador in Holland to find Brewster and put him in prison. The printing office was searched; the types, books, and papers were seized; and Brewster's partner was brought back to England. But Brewster was in England already, keeping out of the attention of the authorities, but engaged in the arrangements of a great plan.

The congregation had now been in Holland for nine years, and the time was coming when the long truce between the Netherlands and Spain would be ended. The old war might be resumed. It seemed to Brewster and the other leaders that it would be wise to make a new removal. Their children were growing up in that strange land, in the midst of many temptations, and might lose their nationality and their religion together. They desired "to live under the protection of England, and to retain the language and the name of Englishmen." They began to propose to themselves the possibility of seeking a new country, in some land unsettled, even uninhabited, where they might establish themselves as a new people, beyond the seas. The history of the English colonies in America had been a tragic one. Again and again, the attempt had been made to gain a place along the Atlantic coast; and again and again the attempt had failed. The Spaniards or the Indians or starvation or cold or fever had destroyed the colony. But in 1607, such a settlement had been securely made in Virginia, at Jamestown. Englishmen, in the face of all these perils combined, had succeeded in living there. The exiles in Holland were disposed to try their fortune.

They knew very well that the dangers were great. They must encounter first the wide sea; then famine and sickness, and the hardships of a strange climate, and then the savages. They were informed that it was the custom of the Indians not only to kill their enemies, but to torture them, to roast them alive and eat their flesh. Still, they would venture.

Brewster, in England, was arranging for this momentous journey. When' he returned to Leyden, he brought with him a grant from the Virginia Company of London, permitting them to settle on lands which they were undertaking to colonize, and assuring them of the good-will of the king. As for James he thought that the farther away they went, the better. The congregation " sought the Lord by a public and solemn fast," and decided that some of them, at least, should go. They desired that their ruling elder should go with them as their spiritual guide, and to this he agreed. They sold their possessions and bought a ship, the *Speedwell,* and hired another ship, the *Mayflower.*

Robinson, their pastor, who was to remain at Leyden, addressed the pilgrims. "Being now ere long to part asunder, and the Lord knowing whether ever he should live to see our faces again, he charged us before God and His blessed angels, to follow him no further than he followed Christ: and if God should reveal anything to us by any other instrument of His, to be as ready to receive it as ever we were to receive any truth by his ministry; for he was very confident that the Lord had more truth and light yet to break forth out of His Holy Word." In the spirit of these noble words, they took their departure.

They went from Leyden to Delft Haven on the sea. "Loath to separate, yet the wind being fair, and the tide admonishing, their pastor falls down upon his knees, and they all with him, while he, with watery cheeks, commends them most fervently to the Lord and His blessing."

It is the scene which is painted in the rotunda of the Capitol at Washington. The man in the center of the group, holding an open Bible in his hands, is William Brewster.

In England, at Southampton, they found the *Mayflower,* and additional companions ready to embark. So out they went, a hundred and twenty passengers, in the two ships. Hardly had they put out to sea, when the *Speedwell* sprung a leak, and back they came for repairs. Again they started, and again after three hundred miles of rough water, the *Speedwell* sprung another leak. They returned to England, put in at the harbor of Plymouth, abandoned the *Speedwell,* and set out at last, with twenty less passengers, in the *Mayflower.* One time, in a fierce storm, a main beam amidships cracked, and only by means of a great iron screw which one of them had brought from Holland was the vessel saved. After a voyage of two months, they came in sight of land.

But the land was the long beckoning arm of Cape Cod, far north of the district named in their grant. They set sail again for the south, but the winds and waves were contrary. At last they landed in the harbor now called Provincetown. In the cabin of the *Mayflower,* before they went ashore, they made and signed a sacred compact. "We," they said, "do, by these presents, solemnly and mutually, in the presence of God and one another, covenant and combine ourselves together into a civil body politic, for our better ordering and preservation; and by virtue hereof, do enact, constitute, and frame such just and equal laws, ordinances, and constitutions and officers, from time to time, as shall be thought most meet and convenient for the general good of the colony; unto which we promise all due submission and obedience." The fourth name signed to this paper was that of William Brewster.

An exploring party was sent to find a location for a settlement, and on the 21st of December, 1620, they came into the harbor which is now called Plymouth, and found there what seemed to them an excellent place for their residence. Making report to the main company at Provincetown, they all moved forward and took possession of the land. There they found sweet springs and running brooks, and a hill on which to set their guns. They set to work to build houses. Already the winter had come on, with cold and storms. The hardships of the new life proved too severe for many of the pilgrims. They fell sick, until "the living were scarce able to bury the dead," and of all the company only seven were well. One of these was Brewster, and the record of those days notes how he and Miles Standish nursed their companions, making their fires, cooking their food, ministering to them in their distress, "and all this willingly and cheerfully, showing herein their true love unto their brethren."

Spring came, and with it appeared the Indians. But they proved to be more peaceable neighbors than had been feared in Holland. They had been visited by a great plague which had reduced their numbers and broken their spirit. When the pilgrims ventured into the forest, they found the bones of those who had thus died. Moreover the friendly Indians warned their companions who were not so friendly that the white men had some more of that same plague bottled up, and would let it out unless they treated them well. Even so, there were alarms, and times of peril, through which Captain Standish carried them safely.

Meanwhile, Brewster was the minister of the congregation. He preached twice on Sunday, and was "very plain and distinct in what he taught" and of "grave and deliberate utterance." On the hill they made a church of thick planks, and on the flat roof set their six cannon. One who visited them said, "They assemble by beat of drum, each with his musket or firelock, in front of the captain's door; they have their cloaks on, and place themselves in order three abreast, and are led by a sergeant without beat of drum. Behind comes the governor, in a long robe; beside him, on the right hand, comes the preacher, with his cloak on, and on the left hand, the captain, with his side arms and cloak, and with a small cane in his hand; and thus they march in good order, and each sets his arms down near him. Thus they enter their place of worship, constantly on their guard, night and day."

Thus the years passed, and the colony prospered. Ships came bringing more settlers; bringing books, also, from time to time, for Brewster's library, till he had four hundred, there in the woods, some in Latin, some in Greek and Hebrew. From Plymouth, the settlement spread to Duxbury. Presently, in Salem and Boston, another settlement was made, and the pilgrims had good English neighbors, sober Puritans.

When Brewster died at the age of eighty-four, he knew that the community which he had led across the sea, and in all whose plans he had had a determining voice, had become an abiding colony. Founded in the name of God, based upon the principle of liberty in religion, making its own laws, and living according to Brewster's precepts, it was the beginning of New England. It was also the beginning,—with the colony at Jamestown,— of the United States of America.

WILLIAM LAUD
From the Painting by H. Stone after Sir A. Van Dyck in National Portrait Gallery LAUD 1573-1645

Sometimes the saints hated the saints. There were good men on both sides, as there are heroes on both sides in all the wars. But it was hard for the good men who were on one side to believe that the good men on the other side were good: they seemed to them to be the enemies of the right.

For the right is almost always made up of two quite different parts, either of which without the other is wrong.

Thus the earth keeps its even course around the sun by the action of those two forces which are called centrifugal and centripetal. If the centrifugal force acted by itself without the centripetal, the earth would fly away into space and be burned up among the stars. If the centripetal force acted by itself without the centrifugal, the earth would be pulled straight into the white hot sun. The earth goes quietly upon its way because both of these forces act together.

So it is with our life. One of the great right things is liberty, and another of the great right things is order. If we have liberty without order, and everybody does whatever he wishes to do, and there are no laws, everything falls into confusion: society becomes like a family in which none of the children obeys his father or mother. If we have order without liberty, and nobody may have his own way, and no experiments may be tried, and no changes may be made, people become like prisoners in a jail. The world of men goes quietly along when liberty and order are in even balance.

Now the Middle Ages were centuries of order. There were strong nations with kings upon their thrones, and the kings said to the people, "All that you have to do is to mind what we say." There was a great, strong Church with a pope ruling over it, and the pope said to the people, "You do not need to think; I will do your thinking for you. Your part is to believe what I tell you." And while the people were barbarous and ignorant, all this was excellent.

But the Reformation brought in the centuries of liberty. Men began to govern themselves without regard to the commands of kings, and they began to think for themselves without regard to the instructions of popes. In the light of this new liberty, they began to see that both popes and kings had often been mistaken, and had been on the side of wrong instead of on the side of right. And the result was that some of them rejected the old order altogether. Thus Luther and Calvin declared their independence of the ancient Church, and proceeded to make new churches according to their own ideas. And they were followed by men who cared even less than they did for the old order. They were on the side of liberty. They proposed to do whatever they thought best.

And, as in the Middle Ages, there were men, like Wycliffe and Hus, who tried to bring liberty into the midst of order, so in the new times, which began with the Reformation, there were men who tried to keep the rule of order in the midst of the new liberty. These men felt that there was too much liberty. They believed in liberty, but they believed also in law. They were afraid of confusion. They were unwilling to have all the old customs abandoned. They wished to bring whatever was good in the past into the present. They tried to keep their neighbors from going too fast and too far.

Thus there were two parties, as there always are, the party of liberty and the party of order. And they contended, as they always do. And the saints who were on the side of liberty hated the saints who were on the side of order; and the saints who believed in order hated the saints who believed in liberty. For example, William Brewster, who held that every community of Christian men should be free to choose its own ministers, and to make its own creed, and to say its prayers in its own way, saw nothing good in the men who as bishops and archbishops were trying to keep the old order in England, and to preserve the old customs, and to maintain the old Church.

Such a man was William Laud.

Laud disliked the Puritans. He disliked them because they offended his sense of order. They refused to go quietly to church like other people, and held meetings in their own houses. This, it is true, was because the bishops would not let them change the services to suit themselves. The bishops would not let them wear their ordinary coats instead of the surplice, nor pray their own prayers instead of those which were provided in the book. Laud stood for the fine and necessary principle of order, as Brewster stood for the fine and necessary principle of liberty.

The England of Laud's time was growing every day more Puritan. The number of people who believed in the doctrines and customs of Calvin, and admired Knox, and wished to change the Church so as to make it as unlike the Mediaeval Church as possible, increased continually. King James, indeed, had disliked the Puritans as heartily as Laud ever did, and had done his best to discourage them. And King Charles, when he came to his father's throne, was of the same mind. The bishops in defense of law and order had turned many of the Puritan clergy out of their places, and had made England an uncomfortable residence for Puritan people. Many had sought refuge across the ocean in New England. But the times were steadily changing, and kings and bishops were as powerless against the new ideas as if they had stood with brooms on the shore of the sea and tried to sweep back the tide. The day came, indeed, when the tide turned, and the party of order got the better of the party of liberty, but not in the lifetime of Laud. He stood against the convictions of a majority of the English people. He was the leader of a lost cause, like one who tries to defend an ancient fortress, and is driven back from one hold to another, and at last dies fighting in the midst of defeat.

For ten years after his graduation at Oxford, Laud was president of one of the colleges of that university, St. John's. Already the Puritans perceived that he was a man of growing power and influence, and that he was against them; and when he was declared elected to the presidency one zealous Puritan not only protested, but tore up the voting papers, so that the matter had to be referred to the king. It is remembered, however, that Laud not only made a good president, but that he was particularly friendly toward the young Puritan who so violently opposed him. When he became bishop of London, he made his opponent president of St. John's College.

Laud was always a devoted friend of the University of Oxford. He never forgot the pleasant years which he spent there as student and master. He loved learning and learned men, and desired to have the pulpits of the Church of

England occupied by scholars. Every year he sent books and manuscripts of value to the library of his old college. When he became great and rich, one of the first things which he did was to erect new buildings for St. John's. The king and queen came to the dedication of these buildings, and were welcomed with speeches and music; a play was acted in their honor; and a mighty feast was served in which the baked meats were shaped by the cook into the forms of archbishops, and bishops, and doctors of divinity.

When Laud became Chancellor of the University he brought into its affairs the same spirit of order which was characteristic of him in all his dealings. He had an account sent him every week of the condition of the colleges, kept professors diligent in their duties, attended to the discipline of students, brought in new teachers, made new laws. Nothing was too small for his attention. "Particularly I pray," he says, "see that none, youth or other, be suffered to go in boots or spurs, or to wear their hair indecently long, or with a lock in the present fashion, or with slashed doublets, or in any light or garish colors." He was at that time one of the busiest men in England, yet he concerned himself with the fashion in which the college students had their hair cut. It illustrates that sense of order to which no details are insignificant.

In 1621, Laud was made a bishop. In 1625, Charles the First became king of England, and made Laud one of his chief advisers. In 1628, he became bishop of London. He now set out to do for the Church of England what he was doing so well for the University of Oxford. He found the nation filled with confusion in religion. Puritans were making experiments in church services, and using the prayer-book, or not using it, as they liked. Laud felt about it as a schoolmaster feels about disorder in his school. He proposed to establish discipline, to have the rules obeyed, and to punish those who were unwilling to obey them.

This was all very unpleasant for the Puritans, who liked their new ways better than the old, and who felt that Laud was interfering with their rightful freedom. No doubt, it would have been better to have allowed more liberty. It would have been better to have permitted the Puritans, so many of whom were grave and devout men, to make some of the changes which they desired in the worship of the Church. It is easy to see that at this long distance of time. Laud did not see it. To him the Puritan novelties were simply interferences with order. Sometimes in school the pupils are wiser than the teachers and ought to have the liberty which they demand: but not often. And whether the pupils are in the right or not, the teachers are apt to judge according to the teachers' point Of view. That is what Laud did. He was an earnest, faithful, Christian man who thought that a bishop, like a schoolmaster, ought to keep people in order.

In 1633, he became Archbishop of Canterbury, and was thus in a position to give commands to the English clergy. To him was committed, so he felt, the care of all the churches.

At that time there was a good deal of debate as to the right place in which the communion table should stand. The Puritans wished to have it down in the church, a plain table like any other, according to their belief that the Holy Communion was simply the Lord's Supper, where bread and wine were eaten and drunk in remembrance of Him. Laud and those who agreed with him wished to have it at the end of the church against the wall, where the altar had always stood, according to their belief that the Holy Communion was an act of worship, the offering of a sacrifice of praise and adoration. It was intolerable to Laud that the Holy Table should be taken out of its ancient, accustomed place, and brought down among the people, where sometimes men sat upon it. It was not only against his idea of the meaning of the sacrament, but against his sense of order. He ordered that the tables should be put back in the chancels.

The same care which he had used at Oxford regarding the conduct of the students, and the fashions of their dress, he now used regarding the conduct of the clergy. He required every minister to wear a surplice when he officiated in the church, in spite of the fact that the clergy who were of the Puritan opinions wished to wear their coats, or black gowns like Calvin. He required every minister to read the services out of the prayer-book, just as they were set down there, without omission or addition. Those who disobeyed, he turned out of their parishes: as a schoolmaster would dismiss a disobedient pupil, or a captain would punish a soldier who refused to wear the uniform of the regiment.

In all this, there was more than a sense of order. Laud perceived that religion in England had come through the Reformation without breaking with the past. The Church government had continued out of the old time into the new, with little change other than that involved in making the clergy subjects of the king instead of subjects of the pope. The worship had likewise continued, with little change other than that involved in translating the services out of Latin into English. The church in which Laud was archbishop was the same church in which Anselm and Becket had occupied the same position. This continuous life was represented by the bishops, whom the Puritans wished to reject, and in lesser ways by the surplice and the book of prayers. The purpose of Laud in insisting on the old customs was to keep the Church of his time in union with the Church of all the former ages. The difference between him and the Puritans was like a debate as to what to do with an ancient church building. The Puritans said, "Pull it all down, and let us build a new one in the new style." Laud said, "Repair it, keep it."

Matters came to a crisis in Scotland. John Knox was dead, but his spirit lived in the hearts of his people. He had made Scotland a Presbyterian country, in whose religion there was neither a bishop nor a prayer-book. King James, indeed, had brought the bishops back, little by little; but neither the bishops nor the king had ventured to bring back the book. The prayers in all the churches were prayed in the minister's own words, and the service was like that which Knox had found in Geneva. To the Scots the bishop and the book,—but especially the book,—meant the old bondage and superstition from which Knox had set them free.

Now one of the defects of the people who have a keen sense of order is a disregard of human nature. They are sure that the thing which they desire is right, and they propose to have it whether men like it or not. They do not stop to ask whether the thing is best for the people under the present conditions, nor do they consider whether the people may be patiently persuaded to accept it, rather than compelled to accept it against their will.

Thus there are sometimes fathers and mothers who insist that all the rooms in the house shall be kept in perfect order, without regard to the fact that children are children. Boys and girls are disorderly by nature. They leave things lying about, because they are made that way. And this must be taken into account. Children must not be treated as if they were forty years of age.

Also there are people who have an idea that they can get their neighbors to do what they like by saying "You must." That is the proper thing to say to children. But when one grown man says it to another grown man who is as good and as wise and as old as he is, the natural reply is "I will not." It makes little difference whether the thing commanded is bad or good. The man resents being ordered about by one who has no right to give him orders. For that is human nature, and must be taken into account by all who would change the ways of their neighbors. People who are forty years of age must not be treated like children.

These two things Laud did not understand. The one thing which was clear to his mind was that the prayer-book was both ancient and excellent, and that all good people in Scotland as well as in England, ought to use it. He did not consider that the Scotch were different from the English, and had had a different religious experience. Neither did he consider that, whether Scotch or English, men will change their minds not by compulsion but by persuasion; he did not understand that when he said " You must," they would instinctively say "No."

So he proposed to introduce the English prayer-book into the Scotch churches. The book was prepared and the day was set when it must be used. And on that day in St. Giles's Church in Edinburgh, the minister began to read the service. The church was filled with people, and the hearts of the people were filled with resentment. Then up rose a stout woman named Jenny Geddes, and flung her kneeling-stool across the church at the minister's head. Immediately the people were in an uproar and the service proceeded no further. The attempt to force the book upon the people failed. All over Scotland, they refused to listen to it. And not only that, but Laud's mistake was like a lighted match applied to a pile which had been heaped high for burning. The nation rose in rebellion. A paper called the Covenant was passed about for signature in all the towns, declaring that the signers would resist all attacks upon the liberty of Scotland. And the Covenanters were formed into an army, and marched on England. And in England multitudes of men who were on the side of liberty sympathized with them. All were against Laud.

One night Laud found his picture, which Vandyke had painted, " fallen down upon the face, and lying on the floor, the string being broken by which it hanged against the wall." He took it as an omen of disaster. One Sunday, five hundred rioters attacked his house, seeking to kill him, but he escaped. Then the Parliament, which was now largely composed of Puritans, impeached him of high treason. That day in the psalms which were said in the service he noted the words: "Blessed is the man whom thou chastenest, O Lord, and teachest him in thy law, that thou mayest give him patience in time of adversity." And in his book of private prayers he wrote: "O eternal God and merciful Father, I humbly beseech thee to look down upon me in this time of my great and grievous affliction. Lord, if it be thy blessed will, make mine innocency appear, and free both me and my profession from all scandal thus raised on me. And howsoever, if thou be pleased to try me to the uttermost, I humbly beseech thee give me full patience, proportionable comfort, contentment with whatsoever thou sendest, and an heart ready to die for thine honor, the king's happiness, and the Church's preservation. And my zeal to these is all the sin yet known to me in this particular for which I thus suffer."

He was taken to the Tower. And outside, the great uprising continued and increased whereby the party of liberty overcame and overturned the party of or der. Charges were formally made against him: thus and thus had he done. But the real charge was that he stood for the old ways. He was for the king and the Church. They took away his books and papers, even his book of private prayers. They must "needs see," he said, "what passed between God and me." They read his diary. Even so, after a long and bitter trial, no ground was discovered on which the accusation of treason could be fairly based. He had, indeed, made mistakes. He had been severe against all Puritan disregard of the customs of the Church. He had kept order, like a strict schoolmaster. He had brought on the Scotch rebellion. But his real offense was leadership of a lost cause. The cause, for the time, was lost, and the leader perished with it. On the same day in which Laud was condemned to death, the Book of Common Prayer was forbidden in England. The House of Commons made the use of it in any church or by any person an offense to be punished by the law.

On the scaffold where he was beheaded Laud stated in a single sentence the purpose for which he had lived. "What clamors and slanders I have endured," he said, "for laboring to keep a uniformity in the external service of God, according to the doctrine and discipline of this Church, all men know and I have abundantly felt." It was not the highest of ideals,—"to keep a uniformity in the external service of God according to the doctrine and discipline of this church"; but it expressed the honest conviction of an honest and devout man. Laud believed that religion thrives best under the quiet conditions of reverent order. In the endeavor to secure such order he died a martyr.

CROMWELL
1599-1658

WHEN Oliver Cromwell was a little lad of four, his godfather, Sir Oliver, entertained the king. The great house of Hinchinbrook was filled with gay courtiers. There was much eating and much drinking. From the University of Cambridge in the neighborhood came grave scholars who addressed his Majesty in the Latin language. The town of Huntingdon, a mile away, gave him a sword of honor. So there was beat of drums, and blare of trumpets, and shining of armor; and the lad looked on with admiration. It was the first great event in his life.

It is said that the next year the prince was brought to Hinchinbrook,—young Charles, who was to be king of England by-and-by. He was four and Oliver was five. The two boys played together, while their elders talked, and the play became so vigorous that at last Oliver knocked Charles down. The little prince was brought in crying. Whether this happened or not, it is altogether likely that Charles and Oliver, who were afterwards to wage so fierce a war and to divide all England into hostile camps, met as children in the great house of Hinchinbrook. And if they did fall to fighting, in those early years, Oliver probably got the better of Charles. He was a sturdy lad, with a quick temper.

Cromwell was twelve years old when there appeared that translation of the Bible into English which is called the King James Version. Everybody was reading it, especially the Puritans. In those days people's houses were not filled with little books and cheap papers as they are now. Shakespeare was near the end of his life, dying in 1616; Milton was born in 1608. Two of Cromwell's favorite books, in later years, were Raleigh's " History of the World," and the "Theatre of God's Judgments," by Dr. Beard, who had been his pastor and tutor. For most persons, reading was a serious matter. Most of the books had large pages, and many of them. Scholars studied huge folios, bigger than the volumes of an encyclopedia.

Into such an age, the English Bible came as a new book. It was read not only with reverence as the Word of God, but with profound interest. Young Oliver discovered in it not only saints but heroes; it was a book of adventure, of conquest, of fighting knights, of brave men who gave their lives in defense of truth and right. He read it, and re-read it. It was his whole library. Much of it he knew by heart. The great sentences of it came easily to his memory. All his life, he spoke the language of the Bible.

And all his life, he thought in the manner of the Bible. God was as real to him as ever He was to the captains and leaders of Israel. When he prayed, he spoke to God as directly and naturally and urgently as Moses and Isaiah did. He believed with all his heart that God was concerned with every act of his life. When he was about to fight a battle, he spent hours of the night before with God, asking the divine advice and help, and he felt that this was of as much importance as all the preparation of the army. When he won a victory,—as he always did, for he never lost a battle in his life,—he was just as sure that God had won it for him as Joshua was when he conquered the Canaanites. And he said so, plainly and naturally. The time came when men talked in this pious way because it was the fashion, and it was connected with hypocrisy, but there was no hypocrisy in Cromwell. If he spoke like Joshua it was because he was in the spirit of Joshua, and regarded the world in the same way as God's world. He wrote from the field, after a series of successes, "The Lord grant that these mercies may be acknowledged with all thankfulness: God exceedingly abounds in His goodness to us, and will not be weary until righteousness and peace meet, and until He hath brought forth a glorious work for the happiness of this poor kingdom." That was in 1645, the year in which Laud died praying for the happiness of the king and the preservation of the Church. Cromwell was engaged in fighting the king and in trying to destroy the Church. But the general spoke as religiously as the archbishop, and was quite as sure that he was doing the will of God.

This is to be kept in mind in any endeavor to understand Cromwell. He has been praised as the greatest soldier and the greatest statesman in the history of England, but he would have said in deep sincerity that all that he did was done for the glory of God, and by the might of God. He lived in the consciousness of the presence of God.

The time passed very quietly for Cromwell till he was over forty years of age. His father died when he was eighteen, and he came home from college to manage the family estate. He carried on the farm at Huntingdon. There he was married, in his twenty-second year. Thirty years after he wrote to his wife, "Thou art dearer to me than any creature "; and she wrote to him, "Truly my life is but half a life in your absence." From Huntingdon, he moved to Ely where his uncle, Sir Thomas Steward, had left him a farm. In both places he was a substantial person among his neighbors.

It is remembered of him that twice a day he gathered his laboring men about him and had prayers with them; and that his house was a refuge for persecuted Puritan ministers. When they were cast out of their parishes, they came to him and he helped them. It is remembered also that he had times of deep depression, and was much troubled about his soul and about the world around him. In all his portraits there is a look of sadness in his eyes, such as one sees in the portraits of Lincoln.

Thus he lived till he was forty-two years old, prosperous, deeply religious in the Puritan manner, tender-hearted to all who were in any trouble, and taking life seriously.

Meanwhile the conservatives, the party of order, and the progressives, the party of liberty, were entering into that contention in the course of which Laud lost his life. The party of order was represented by the king and his court, and by the bishops and the Church. The party of liberty was represented by the House of Commons, and by the Puritan ministers. Thus the contention was both political and religious.

On the political side the question was whether England should be governed by a king who might do as he pleased, or by a king who should act according to the wishes of the people as expressed by their representatives in Parliament. On the side of Charles it was to be said that all the kings of England had ruled the country at their own pleasure. The people, it is true, had sometimes risen in opposition to the king; as, for example, when they made John sign the Great Charter. But the theory remained that the king owned England. This theory Charles had inherited from his father. It was the old, orderly method of government; thus had things proceeded from times immemorial; this was what it meant to be a king. And to this theory the bishops and the church people generally agreed; not only because the king was on their side, but because they inclined naturally to the old ways.

It was plain, however, to many people that the old ways were bad. The king as supreme did things which the people did not like. Sometimes he carried the nation into foolish wars. Often he took the money which the people paid in taxes and spent it on himself or his favorites, or in a manner which did no good to the country. In the midst of the debates about religion he held the position that all the people ought to believe as he did, and when they said that their consciences would not allow them to do that, he undertook to compel them. Thus he aroused against him both the patriotic citizens, who saw that he was misgoverning the country, and the Puritans whose religion he opposed.

The contention came to a crisis when the king wanted money, and directed the Parliament to get it for him by taxes, and the Parliament told him that they would not vote a penny until they knew what he intended to do with it, and were satisfied that it was a good thing to do. Charles tried to get the money by taxing the people himself, but Cromwell's cousin, John Hampden, became the leader of the people in refusing to pay. Charles called the Parliament together, and when they refused to vote supplies until he agreed to do what they demanded in Church and state he dismissed them.

At last, in 1640, a Parliament was assembled which refused to be dismissed. It continued in session for thirteen years, and is called the Long Parliament on that account. The immediate business of this Parliament was to make plain to the nation that England was unbearably misgoverned both in politics and in religion. It set out to compel the king to give up his supreme authority in the state, and to change the Church of England so that it should be no longer Episcopal but Presbyterian.

In 1642 the king assembled an army on his side, and the Parliament assembled an army on their side, and a civil war began. For the most part the upper and the lower classes were for the king — the nobles and the peasants, the aristocratic and cultivated people, the bishops and the clergy, the professors and students of Oxford and Cambridge, and the inhabitants of the villages, the men who tilled the ground. For the most part, the middle classes were for the Parliament,—the merchants, the lawyers, the lesser gentry, the inhabitants of the great towns, the city of London. Geographically, the north and west sided with the king; the south and east, with the Parliament.

Into this war, Oliver Cromwell entered with all his might. At first he was the captain of a company of his neighbors; then the colonel of a regiment; then a general of cavalry. At the beginning, he knew no more about war than any shopkeeper in Ely; but two things became plain to him. He saw that battles were decided, in the first place, by the spirit of the men. The king's men were gentlemen, who had "honor and courage and resolution in them"; they fought like knights. Cromwell sought out men who should meet this might of chivalry with the might of religion. "I raised such men," he said, "as had the fear of God before them, as made some conscience of what they did." One who observed them said, "He had a special care to get religious men into his troop." They were sober; they were profoundly in earnest; they were devoted to the cause in which they fought as the cause of God.

Cromwell saw also that battles are decided, in the second place, by men who have not only spirit but discipline. He drilled them. He taught them by continual exercise how to handle their horses and themselves. He trained them in the art of war. Thus his mounted men, who came presently to be known as the Ironsides, learned that the first step towards victory is obedience. They could be counted on to respond instantly to the word of command. Instead of being so many hundred men each fighting his own battles in his own way, they became an army. Their force when they charged was like the force of a cannonball. In the great and awful game of war, they met their opponents as a trained team in football plunges through an untrained team. No such disciplined and effective soldiers had been seen in Europe since Caesar led his legions into Gaul.

These men, thus made strong by conscience and by discipline, defeated the armies of the king. First at Marston Moor, in 1644, Cromwell destroyed the king's forces in the north; then, in 1645, at Naseby, he destroyed the king's forces in the south.

Between these two battles he fought and won another, almost as important, in the discussions of the Parliament.

The Puritans in Parliament were of two parties, Presbyterian and Independent. The Presbyterians were conservative. They desired to make changes in religion, but not to permit any great individual liberty. They proposed to make England a Presbyterian nation, and they intended to compel everybody to be Presbyterians like themselves. The Independents were of William Brewster's way of thinking, and would allow most men to think for themselves in religion and to act in accordance with their thought.

The religious differences entered into the conduct of the war. The Presbyterians were afraid of going too far. They wished to beat the king, but not too severely. They dreaded the progress of the rebellion. The Earl of Manchester, whom the Parliament had put in charge of the war, said, "If we beat the king ninety and nine times, yet he is king still, and so will his posterity be after him." He had the old reverence for kings. He was a Presbyterian. But Cromwell was reported to have said that "if he met the king in battle, he would fire his pistol at him as at another." Cromwell was an Independent. Under the Presbyterian conditions the war might go on forever.

Then Cromwell proposed that the army should be reorganized, and that in the place of companies of militia there should be one united force, under one commander, and under such discipline as was used by the Ironsides. At the same time it was proposed that all the present generals who were also members of Parliament should resign, and leave the control of the army to men who were neither politicians nor Parliamentarians, but soldiers. After long debate, these proposals were adopted: the Earl of Manchester with his half-hearted policy gave up his position; and the new army, at Naseby, destroyed the army of the king.

These changes, however, had another and very important result. They not only made the army strong enough to conquer the king, but they made it independent of the Parliament.

Thus there were three parties in the nation: the Royalists, who wished to restore the king to power, and to make the religion of England Episcopal again; the Presbyterians, who composed the majority in the Parliament, and were disposed to come to terms with the king, if only they might make the religion of England Presbyterian; and the army. But the army was composed mainly of Independents, or as we now say, Congregationalists, who were resolved that England should be neither exclusively Episcopal nor exclusively Presbyterian, but that every man should be free to follow his own religious convictions, so long as he gave the same freedom to his neighbor. The chief man in the army was Cromwell. He had been kept in command when the other Parliamentary generals resigned, because they could not get along without him.

The king was conquered, but the king's friends were many. Especially in Scotland, the Royalists were strong. The Scotch Presbyterians were in sympathy with the English Presbyterians who held the power in Parliament. Both were encouraged to believe that the king, if he were again upon his throne, would side with them. Armies began to gather in the north of England. Out of Scotland, twenty thousand men under the Duke of Hamilton began to march down over the border. The whole war which had seemed to be decided at Marston Moor and Naseby must be fought over again. Cromwell fought it in one battle. At Preston, in 1648, he fell suddenly upon the forces under Hamilton and destroyed them almost before they knew by whom they were attacked.

It was now clear to Cromwell that there were two chief hindrances to the peace and freedom of England; one was the Parliament, the other was the king. So long as these two continued in power, they would stir up civil war; and the victory of either of them, or of both together, would be the end of religious liberty. The supremacy of the king would mean an Episcopal despotism; the supremacy of the Parliament would mean a Presbyterian despotism. Cromwell and the army were determined that England should be politically and religiously free. Cromwell felt that he was raised up for that purpose by the hand of God.

Thereupon the first thing which he did after the battle of Preston was to take away the power of the Parliament. On Wednesday, the 6th of December, 1648, the members of that body, coming to the daily session, found Colonel Pride's regiment stationed at the door, and every objectionable member was turned back. Those only were admitted who were willing to obey the army. And the next thing which was done was to try, and condemn, and behead the king. In January 1649, this tremendous step was taken. Thus the two representatives of the ancient order, the two legal means of government, the king and the Parliament were done away. The power was in the hands of the army, and the head of the army was Oliver Cromwell.

Cromwell ruled England for ten years. There were insurrections in various parts of the country, notably in Ireland, but he put them down with a strong hand. There were continual plots against his life, but he escaped them all. There was at first the universal opposition of the monarchies of Europe against the English gentleman and soldier who had killed a king, and seated himself upon his throne, but all this changed into respect. The ruler of England was never so strong in Europe, the navy of England was never so powerful on the seas, as in the days of Cromwell. And the nation itself had never been so prosperous or substantially peaceful; never had justice been administered so fairly; never had men in office been so honest or so intent upon the public welfare. Never had there been a court in England or in Europe with such simplicity of life, in which bad men were so out of favor and good men were so cherished. The nation was ruled, during the ten years of Cromwell's reign, upon the principles of religion.

Once again during this time, he had to fight the king. The king was dead, but as the Earl of Manchester predicted, he still lived in the person of his son. The Royalists, in spite of Marston Moor and Naseby, and in spite of Preston, raised still another army, and they were joined by a great host from Scotland. Cromwell went up to meet the Scots. At the battle of Dunbar, against great odds, he defeated them with a decisive defeat; and at Worcester he cut to pieces the Royalists who had joined Charles, and drove him out of England.

Also, in Cromwell's reign, he had trouble again with Parliament. He believed that the right way to govern the country was, as he expressed it, by a Single Person and a Parliament. The Single Person was to be the executive officer, the Parliament was to make laws and levy taxes. He believed also that the government ought to have a constitution, a written statement of fundamental principles, according to which both the Single Person and the Parliament must conduct themselves. But in these beliefs the Parliament did not share. They desired more power. Cromwell came into the Long Parliament and turned it out of doors. "You are no Parliament," he said. And that was true, for they had ceased to be the representatives of the people. "I say," he repeated, " you are no Parliament. Come, come, we have had enough of this. I will put an end to your prating. " He called a national assembly which is remembered as the Par-liament of the Saints: they were all leaders of religion. But the Saints had wild and impracticable notions about the welfare of the country, and no knowledge of the art of government. Cromwell had to send them home. And so it was with another Parliament, and yet another. Cromwell's great ideas were adopted at last, years after, when the English colonies in America became the United States, under a President and a Congress, and according to a constitution. But in his own time he found the Parliament as difficult to work with as ever Charles had done. His only way was to rule by his own wisdom.

Thus he was supreme in England, and was king in all but name. He was called the Lord Protector, and the nation which had been a monarchy was called the Commonwealth. And he reigned in peace and righteousness until his life's end. He made England free. Out of the old order of things which had existed since the beginning of history, wherein the prince had possessed the power of the state, he brought the nation into our modern time, wherein the power is in the possession of the people. He was the pioneer of all the republics. He shares with William the Silent the glory of leading the great march of liberty.

There was a debate in Anselm's time as to whether a certain good man ought to be called a saint, because he had given his life, not in defense of the Church nor in the cause of religion, but on behalf of the people, protesting against an unjust tax. "Yes, he was a saint indeed," said Anselm, "because he died for liberty; and the cause of liberty is the cause of God." Thus lived and died Oliver Cromwell, soldier, statesman, and saint, whose honest endeavor in all that he said and did was to fulfil the will of God.

BUNYAN

16z8-i688 JOHN Bunyan was brought up in Puritan England. In Bedford, where he lived, the prevailing religion was of the Puritan kind. His father, indeed, was a tinker, and the boy was taught that trade; and the tinkers were wandering people, like gipsies, who went about from village to village mending pots and kettles and doing odd jobs, and were not much interested in religion. The elder Bunyan, however, seems to have stayed in Bedford; being in that respect unlike most tinkers. And the younger Bunyan, from his earliest youth, was singularly sensitive to religious influences.

The Puritan religion laid great emphasis upon the fact of sin. The Puritans were Calvinists, and believed that all people are born bad, and are under the wrath of God, and are destined to be punished forever in the flames of hell, unless they escape. Some are enabled to escape, by the grace of God, through the mercy gained for sinners by the death of Christ, but they are few in number. Salvation was thought to be a matter of much uncertainty and difficulty. The devil was very real and near, and was constantly endeavoring to get possession of men's souls. Every sin strengthened his hold. People lived in fear; afraid of God, and of the devil, and of the pains of hell. Before John Bunyan was ten years old he dreamed night after night that the devil was running away with him.

To the strict Puritans of Bunyan's time even the innocent pleasures of youth were wrong. Living as men did in a world which was to decide their everlasting condition, out of which they were to go either into hell or into heaven, the main business of life was the proper preparation of the soul. There was no time for the satisfaction of the senses. The world was no place for play or laughter. Even boys and girls must go about with sober faces, and remember that it is appointed to every one to die, and after death the judgment.

Of course, human nature asserted itself, in spite of the Puritan teaching. It is indeed true that life is a serious matter, and that sin is a grievous thing, and that we must be on guard against temptation, and that nothing is so important as right thinking, and right speaking, and right acting. It is true that we must, above all things, do our duty, and heed the voice of conscience. But it is true also that the world is very pleasant, that the sun shines and the birds sing, and that God has given us not only souls but bodies. It is true that God has implanted in us the desire not only to pray but to play, and that we naturally laugh more than we cry because we are made that way.

So there was young John Bunyan, with a strong love for dancing with the girls on the village green, and for joining with the boys in ringing the bells of the village church. He liked to play tip-cat. There was even a novel which he liked to read, called the "History of Sir Bevis of Southampton," a story of knights and ladies and adventures. But as he did these pleasant things, there was in his soul an unhappy feeling that he was doing wrong. One bad habit he certainly had: he was given to swearing. But even this seems to have been a kind of natural protest against the sober piety about him. Whatever was the reason for it, he stopped it when he was rebuked and told how wrong it was.

Thus he lived up to the age of seventeen, a good lad, saying his prayers and reading his Bible, and listening every Sunday to very long sermons, terribly afraid of the devil, and imagining himself—poor little fellow—to be a great sinner. Then King Charles gathered his army together to fight for what he believed to be his rights, and the Parliament gathered an army against him, and the civil war began, and Bunyan became a soldier.

He brought out of this experience a knowledge of battles which he never forgot. The drums and trumpets, the flying banners, the discipline of the camp, the shock of the charge, the noise of guns, the sight of blood and death, illustrated that war which the devil is forever waging against the soul of man. He brought also a new sense of the uncertainty of life. At the siege of a city, one of his companions, who had for the moment taken Bunyan's place, was killed.

He came back out of the wars, and married a wife whose only dowry was a bundle of religious books. These he read, and the reading quickened all his former uneasiness about his sins. One day in the midst of a game of tip-cat, he heard a voice in his soul demanding whether he would leave his sins and go to heaven, or continue in his sins and go to hell. There he stood with his stick uplifted in his hand, staring at the sky. He never played again. He gave up bell-ringing, though he looked on while the other young men pulled the ropes, till he was suddenly seized with an awful fear that the steeple would fall upon his head. He gave up dancing on the green.

For a time, his religious scruples gave him such distress that he seemed in danger of losing his mind. He thought that he had committed the unpardonable sin, though he did not know exactly what it was. He thought that if he had faith, even as a grain of mustard seed, he could dry up all the puddles between Elstow and Bedford. He was assailed day after day with a temptation to sell Christ. Wherever he went, and whatever he did, he heard the devil at his ear whispering, "Sell him. Sell him." At last he cried, "Let him go if he will"; and then he thought that he was lost indeed. Even after these agonies were over, and he began to come out of this valley of the shadow of death, and joined the Baptist church at Bedford, and partook, for the first time, of the Lord's Supper, he was tempted to shock the congregation by swearing aloud. And after he had begun to preach, he felt the devil urging him to say horribly wicked things in the midst of his sermons. Out of these spiritual torments he was brought at last into peace and joy by the suffering of real pain. He was arrested and put in jail at Bedford, and kept there for twelve years.

For Cromwell was now gone, and his son Richard, who for a while reigned in his stead, was not strong enough to govern England, and so Charles the Second was invited to come back and take the throne from which his father had been thrust out. And when the king came back the Church came with him. During Cromwell's time all the ministers in England were Puritans, and all the services were Puritan services. Even in the cathedrals, the prayers of the ministers took the place of the ancient prayers of the book. The Episcopal clergy, who had been turned out of their churches in Queen Mary's time by the Roman Catholics, were now turned out by Presbyterians and Congregationalists. But the king came back, and at once all was changed. It was now the Presbyterians and the Congregationalists who must go. All who were willing to use the prayer-book might remain, but a law was passed that after a certain Sunday, all who were not willing to do that must resign their places. Accordingly, a great many Puritan ministers resigned, nearly two thousand. And not only that, but other laws were passed to prevent them from preaching. For the moment, in the enthusiasm of the return of the king and of the Church, the plans of Laud were taken up again, and it was proposed to compel everybody in England to belong to the Episcopal Church.

For Cromwell's great idea of liberty of conscience was still in advance of the age. Almost all good men believed that it was necessary to decide things in religion one way or the other, and to make everybody submit to the decision. The good man of that time said to himself, "I am right, and my neighbors who do not agree with me are wrong; I must make them do my way." Thus the Presbyterians, if Cromwell had not prevented them, would have passed laws to make England Presbyterian, and to punish, not only Episcopalians, but Congregationalists and Baptists. Thus the Puritans, when they settled in Salem and Boston and began the Commonwealth of Massachusetts, expelled Baptists and whipped Quakers. The idea of uniformity in religion was in most men's minds.

Only a very few great men, like William the Silent and Oliver Cromwell, believed what we all believe now, that men should be allowed to think their own thoughts, and say their own prayers, and arrange their churches in their own way, so long as they do no harm to their neighbors.

Thus when John Bunyan, in defiance of the laws, began to preach without having the permission of a bishop, he was put in jail. The authorities felt that if they allowed uneducated and unordained men to preach, the confusion of the time would be continued. The old order had returned to power, and was putting down the new liberty. They tried to get the tinker to promise that he would not preach; but he felt like the apostles that he was sent from God and must preach, no matter what the laws might be. To jail he went, then.

They laughed at him; they said that the only divine commission which he had was to mend old kettles. They threatened him. "If you break the law," they said, "you will be banished, and if you come back we will hang you by the neck." It was exactly what the Puritans in Boston said to Mary Dyer and other Quakers; and they did banish them and afterwards hang them. Nothing could make Bunyan promise not to preach. "If you let me out to-day," he said, " I will preach again to-morrow."

So there he lay in jail. Jails, even now, are not comfortable places. In Bunyan's time they were hot in summer and bitterly cold in winter, and filthy all the year round. Moreover, being in jail, he was not only separated from his family, but was unable to support them by working at his trade. He knew that his wife and his little children, whom he dearly loved, were hungry because he would not promise not to preach. He thought of his blind daughter, how she had no food and no fire. Even this did not change his resolution. He knew that God commanded him to preach, and preach he would. "I must," he said, "I must do it."

Unable to ply his trade of tinker, Bunyan learned in his prison to make "longtagged thread laces," and sold them. And he preached to his companions in captivity, making the jail a church for those who were confined in it with him. And as he worked, he read. He had two books, the Bible and Foxe's "Book of Martyrs." These he read over and over, till he knew them almost by heart. And presently, he began to write. He was a poor speller, and his grammar was tinker's grammar, but he had certain great advantages which more than made up for these defects.

One of his advantages was an earnest spirit. He wrote solely for the purpose of helping his neighbors, and with as little thought for his own fame or gain as any of the prophets or apostles. He believed that God wished him to preach, and being hindered from preaching with his voice, he preached with his pen. Another of his advantages was an acquaintance with his own soul, and with the souls of other poor people like himself. He had gone through a deep religious experience and had come out of darkness into light, and thus knew the way and was able to be a guide.

Still another advantage was his intimate familiarity with the greatest of all books; for the best education consists in part of experience of life, and in part of knowledge of the thoughts of great thinkers. Bunyan, reading the Bible day and night, learning by heart its history and poetry, associating continually with its sages and saints, and breathing in its divine spirit, was better educated in Bedford jail than any youth of the time who was studying Latin and Greek at Oxford. Thus he wrote the deep thoughts of his own soul in the language of the Bible. Even his imprisonment helped him, for he had time to think and write.

In jail at Bedford, then, this poor tinker began the book which made him famous. "As I walked through the wilderness of this world," he said, " I lighted on a certain place where was a den, and laid me down in that place to sleep." The den was Bedford jail. "And as I slept," he says, " I dreamed a dream. I dreamed, and behold, I saw a man clothed with rags standing in a certain place, with his face from his own house, a book in his hand, and a great burden upon his back. I looked and saw him open the book and read therein; and as he read he wept and trembled; and not being able longer to contain he broke out with a lamentable cry, saying, ' What shall I do?"' Thus begins the Pilgrim's Progress.

The man, whose name was Christian, answered his own question by making his way out of the City of Destruction where he dwelt, and taking his journey through all manner of hindrances and perils to the land of Beulah, and the Mount Zion, and the Celestial City, the heavenly Jerusalem. He tumbled into the Slough of Despond, but struggled out again. He got into trouble by following the advice of Mr. Worldly Wiseman, but was brought back by the aid of Evangelist. He learned useful lessons in the House of the Interpreter. He came upon a cross beside the way, and the burden of his sins fell off. From the heights of the Hill Difficulty, he saw in the far distance, in the midst of Immanuel's Land, the fair slopes of the Delectable Mountains. He did hard but successful battle with the dragon Apollyon, and entered into the Valley of the Shadow of Death. "I thought over and over," he says, " I should have been killed there; but at last the day broke, and the sun rose." He passed the tower of Vanity Fair. In the grounds of Doubting Castle he lay down to sleep, and Giant Despair came out and got him. The Giant put him in a dungeon and beat him with a grievous crab-tree cudgel. At last, says Christian, "What a fool am I thus to lie in an evilsmelling dungeon, when I may as well walk at liberty. I have a key in my bosom, called Promise, that will, I am persuaded, open any lock in Doubting Castle." So out he came, and reached the Delectable Mountains, and came in sight of the Celestial City. He forded a deep river which lay before Mount Zion, and in the shining city all the bells began to ring, and over the gate was written, "Blessed are they that do his commandments that they may have right to the tree of life, and may enter in through the gates into the city." And the gates opened and Christian entered; and "I looked in," says he who dreamed the dream, "and behold, the city shone like the sun; the streets also were paved with gold; and in them walked many men, with crowns on their heads, palms in their hands, and golden harps, to sing praises withal." "And after that, they shut up the gates; which, when I had seen, I wished myself among them."

The "Pilgrim's Progress" came into the hands of people who were hungry for good stories, as all right-minded people are, but who had persuaded themselves that stories are bad reading. They had denied themselves the pleasant company of Sir Bevis of Southampton and of all the other heroes of romance. As for Shakespeare, his wonderful stories were worse than the others because they were plays and the Puritans associated plays with all wickedness. Thus even children, in those days, were growing up without knowing what the delight of stories meant. They had, it is true, the Bible in which were the most marvelous stories which were ever told; but the Bible stories were told so soberly and with so little thought that any child would ever read them that most of the children found them as difficult as the long Sunday sermons. But here, at last, was a book of pious stories, yet not so pious as to be uninteresting; a book about giants and dragons, and adventurous heroes, a fairy tale, which could be read even by Puritans, and even on Sunday!

At first, only poor people read it, Bunyan's neighbors in Bedford and Elstow, and other uneducated persons. It was printed on coarse paper, with queer, cheap pictures. But the fame of it passed from one to another. There was a second edi-. tion, a third, an eighth, a ninth, a tenth. Even before Bunyan died, many thousand copies had been sold, in England, in Scotland, even in France and Holland, even across the ocean in the Puritan colonies. Bunyan wrote a second part, in which Christian's wife and children journeyed over the same road. Other books came from his pen; the "Holy War," an account of the siege of the soul; "Grace Abounding," an account of his own religious life. But "Pilgrim's Progress" stands by itself as not only the best of Bunyan's writings, but as the most popular religious book ever written in the English language.

Bunyan was released from jail, and became so eminent a person that he was called "the bishop of the Baptists." Charles the Second wished for various reasons to favor the Roman Catholics, and he repealed the laws which punished those who would not attend the service of the Church of England. By this repeal all the other dissenters benefited. All the jails were opened, and they who had been convicted, like Bunyan, of having "devilishly and perniciously abstained from coming to church," were set free. Now he might preach as much as he liked. And preach he did, even in London, and in a hundred country towns. One time he went in a pouring rain to persuade an angry father to forgive a disobedient son, and caught a heavy cold of which he died. His grave in Bunhill Fields became a Protestant shrine and place of pilgrimage. His supreme sermon was his great book, in which he lives and preaches still.

GEORGE FOX
From the Painting by Sir Peter Lely at Swarthmore College, Pa.
FOX 1624-1691

George Fox had three inconvenient ideas which kept him in trouble continually.

One idea was that it is wrong to say "you" to a single person. Because, he said, "you" is a plural pronoun. The proper word for a single person is "thee" or "thou." This was innocent enough, but it had the effect of showing everybody that Fox was queer. That appeared in the shortest conversation.

Another idea was that it is wrong for a man to take off his hat as a mark of respect for his neighbors or superiors. In Fox's time people were very elaborately polite. Men wore plumed hats, and took them off with bows which made the plumes touch the ground. It seemed to Fox an artificial and foolish custom, and he would not do it. He kept his hat on even in the presence of the judge in the courtroom. But that which ordinary gentlemen accounted as only the bad manners of a rude fellow from the country, the judges took to be contempt of court.

"Oh! the rage and scorn," says Fox, "the heat and fury that arose! Oh! the blows, punchings, beatings, and imprisonments that we underwent for not putting off our hats to men! For that soon tried all men's patience and sobriety what it was. Some had their hats violently plucked off and thrown away, so that they quite lost them. The bad language and evil usage we received on this account are hard to be expressed, besides the danger we were sometimes in of losing our lives for this matter." Of course, when Fox and his followers were brought into court, as they often were, this curious scruple about their hats prejudiced the judge against them. Sometimes they were put in jail for no other reason than this apparently impertinent defiance of propriety.

The third inconvenient idea was a belief that it is wrong for men to swear. That, of course, is true. But Fox applied if not only to profane oaths but to the appeal to God by which men emphasized their words in courts of justice. Fox quoted the Sermon on the Mount, where the Lord said, "Swear not at all, but let your communication be yea, yea, nay, nay." The result was that whenever he was arrested,—as he often was for disturbing the peace,—he not only angered the judge by coming in with his hat on, but he stopped the proceedings at the very beginning by refusing to take the customary oath.

And that was not the worst of it. The England of Fox's time was filled with contention. The Civil War began when he was eighteen years of age; and after it was ended, and Cromwell became the ruler of the country, there were endless plots to kill him and to bring back the king; and when the tide turned and Charles the Second sat on his father's throne, there were endless plots again in opposition to his oppressive government. The situation affected the nerves of the nation. Every rumor frightened those who heard it. Every unusual movement in the country scared the people like a strange sound late at night. All queer people were suspected of being plotters against Cromwell or against Charles. And the plan which was adopted to discover what the queer people meant was to put them on their oath. "Come," the magistrates said, "swear that you are a true and loyal citizen." But George Fox would not swear.

The consequence was that this strange person who went up and down the counFOX try saying, " thee" and "thou," and wearing his hat, and preaching sermons which nobody could understand, was taken to be a dreadful enemy. People could not make out what he meant, and they mistrusted him of all manner of evil. The judges who served under Cromwell said, "You are a Roman Catholic "; the judges who served under Charles said, "You are a Presbyterian." And, whatever they accused him of, Fox refused to clear himself by the taking of an oath.

Moreover, in those days, when all England was engaged in fighting, Fox would not fight. For to these three inconvenient opinions he added a fourth: he believed that war was wrong. Here again he had on his side the Sermon on the Mount. The Lord said " Love your enemies." But he had against him one of the oldest of all the customs of the world, since the time when Cain struck Abel,—and he found no sympathy for his opinions among religious people. Cromwell's Ironsides prayed longest before they went to battle, and believed that they and the Lord were fighting together for the cause of righteousness and liberty.

Men came to Fox and offered to make him a captain to fight for the Commonwealth against King Charles. "I told them," he says, " I knew from whence all wars did arise, even from the lust, according to James's doctrine; and that I lived in the virtue of that life and power that took away the occasion of all wars. Then their rage got up, and they said, 'Take him away, jailer, and put him into the dungeon amongst the rogues and felons.' So I was had away, and put into a lousy, stinking place, without any bed, amongst thirty felons, where I was kept almost half a year."

Behind these stout convictions of George Fox was his belief in the Inner Light. He heard the voice of God speaking in his soul, telling him what to do and what not to do.

He had come into this belief with difficulty. As a lad, he had kept sheep, like the Prophet Amos, and had thus lived much by himself and had had opportunity to think. "In my very young years," he says, "I had a gravity and staidness of mind and spirit not usual in children." Even as a boy, when he saw that a thing was right he was determined to do it. They who knew him used to say, "If George says verily, there is no altering him." His family thought that he should be a minister, but his father was persuaded by some friends and put him to work with a shoemaker. Thus he lived industriously, and very gravely and soberly, till he was nearly twenty. It was plain that the shoemaker's apprentice was different from the other young men of the village. "When boys and rude people would laugh at me," he says, " I left them alone, and went my way; but people had generally a love to me for my innocency and honesty."

When he was about twenty, he left his trade and his family, and for three or four years wandered about the country, even going into London. He was seeking for religious satisfaction.

England was now, for the most part, a Presbyterian nation, and Fox's ideas of religion were derived from Presbyterian sermons. They did not appeal to him. They were filled with difficult doctrines, and dwelt constantly upon the sinfulness of human nature. Fox talked with the Presbyterian rector of his home parish, but he did him no good. Fox says that the minister would get his sermons out of these conversations. "What I said in discourse to him on the week-days, that he would preach on the first-days, for which I did not like him."

Another minister advised him to smoke tobacco and sing psalms; but "tobacco," he says, "was a thing I did not love, and psalms I was not in a state to sing: I could not sing." To still another minister he went, but " as we were walking together in his garden, the alley being narrow, I chanced, in turning, to set my foot on the side of a bed, at which the man was in a rage as if his house had been on fire."

Thus the ministers, to whom no doubt this grave strange youth was a perplexity, gave him no comfort. One day as he was walking in a field, the Lord "opened" to him that " being bred at Oxford or Cambridge was not enough to fit or qualify men to be ministers of Christ. " Another time, by another "opening," it was disclosed to him that "God who made the world did not live in temples made with hands." In consequence of these new thoughts, he ceased to go to church, but on Sundays wandered in the fields.

Gradually, in the course of his solitary wanderings and his constant reading of the Bible, it was borne in upon the soul of Fox that God was speaking to him, as He spoke in the old time to His people, and that this was a blessing which all people might enjoy if they would.

"I saw," he says, "that Christ died for all men, and enlightened all men and women with His divine and saving light. I saw that I was to bring people off from all the world's religions, which are vain; that they might know the pure religion, might visit the fatherless, the widows and the strangers, and keep themselves from the spots of the world. I was to bring them off from all the world's fellowships, and prayings, and singings, which stood in forms without power. I was to bring people off from Jewish ceremonies and from heathenish fables, and from men's inventions and windy doctrines, by which they blew people about this way and the other way, from sect to sect."

And "these things," he says, "I did not see by the help of man, nor by the letter, though they are written in the letter, but I saw them in the light of the Lord Jesus Christ, and by His immediate spirit and power, as did the holy men of God by whom the Holy Scriptures were written. "

Thus George Fox became a missionary to the Presbyterians and the Episcopalians of England. In the midst of all the Puritan preaching about the wrath of God, he declared the infinite and prevailing love of God. "I saw," he says, "that there was an ocean of darkness and death; but an infinite ocean of light and love, which flowed over the ocean of darkness." In the midst of all the sermons about difficult doctrines, he taught that the essence of religion consists in doing good. And in the midst of all the services and sacraments, he taught that these are only the outsides of religion; he and his followers put them all away, sitting in silence at their meetings unless the Spirit moved one or another to speak or pray.

Fox's belief in the Inner Light took the place of the common reliance of men upon the Bible and the Church. These ancient authorities were of little use to one who heard God speaking in his own soul. One day he came to Nottingham as the bells were ringing for the Sunday service, and as he saw the church, or, as he called it, the "great steeple-house," the Lord said to him, "Thou must go cry against yonder great idol, and against the worshipers therein. " So in he went, "and the priest (like a great lump of earth) stood in his pulpit above." The preacher's text was, "We have also a more sure word of prophecy." This, he said, was the Scriptures, "by which they were to try all doctrines, religions, and opinions." Then the power of the Lord was mighty upon Fox, and he stood up in his place in the congregation and cried, "Oh no, it is not the Scriptures," and he told them what it was, namely, the Holy Spirit by which the Holy Men of God gave forth the Scriptures." That is, he proclaimed the doctrine of the light of God in every man. "As I spake thus amongst them," he says, "the officers came and took me away, and put me into a nasty, stinking prison, the smell whereof got so into my nose and throat that it very much annoyed me."

This was the first of six or eight imprisonments. The common charge was that Fox was a disturber of the peace, and though the punishments were most unjust and out of all proportion to the offense, the charge was true enough. He felt it his mission to attack Presbyterian ministers in their own parishes, and to declare that the customary religion of religious people was a false religion.

One time, he says, "as I was walking, I lifted up my head, and I saw three steeple-house spires, and they struck at my life." He asked what place that was, and was told that it was Lichfield. And the Word of the Lord told him to go thither. "And as soon as I was got within the city, the Word of the Lord came to me again, saying, *I Cry, woe to the bloody city of Lichfield!*' So I went up and down the streets crying with a loud voice, 'Woe to the bloody city of Lichfield!' It being market day, I went into the market place, and to and fro in the several parts of it, and made stands, crying as before, 'Woe to the bloody city of Lichfield.'"

The very strangeness of such behavior attracted attention, and the preacher gathered disciples; some of them queer people whose heads were not quite right, but others grave and substantial persons who heard in the words of Fox a call of God to a spiritual religion. These people came to be called Quakers because they bid their hearers to quake and tremble at the word of the Lord. But they called themselves the Society of Friends. Fox was of a dignified and impressive appearance, wearing his hair long, and looking at people out of very remarkable eyes. "See his eyes!" they cried, as he was speaking. He had an eloquence which made men in taverns stop their drinking to listen to him; so that one time as he preached in a tavern on the Inner Light, the innkeeper, seeing that his business was stopped, thrust a candle into his hand at the first pause, saying, "Come, here is a light for you to go into your chamber." Wherever he went, discussion and disturbance came with him. He made himself a suit of leather, and he says that people trembled when it was told them, "The man in leather breeches is come."

This strange ministry of Fox continued for some forty years. Much of it was in the midst of great excitement and opposition. Much of it was interrupted by imprisonment in horrible jails, where he lived under conditions which would have put a speedy end to the life of any but a very strong man. The dungeon called Doomsdale at Launceston was a foul place, where the prisoners were fed like dogs through a grating. At Lancaster Castle, "I was put," he says, "in a tower, where the smoke of the other prisoners came up so thick that I could hardly see the candle when it burned. Besides, it rained in upon my bed, and many times when I went out to stop the rain in the cold, winter season, my shirt was wet through with the rain that came in upon me while I was laboring to stop it out. And the place being high, and open to the wind, sometimes as fast as I stopped it, the wind blew it out again. In this manner did I lie all that long, cold winter."

All this Fox endured for conscience' sake. He was as certain as any prophet in the Old Testament that he was doing the divine will. He expected suffering, as Jeremiah did; and when it came, he endured it patiently as for the Lord. "Dear Heart," he wrote to his wife, "Thou seemedst to be a little grieved when I was speaking of prisons, and when I was taken: be content with the will of the Lord God. The Lord's power is over all; blessed be His Holy name forever." And, indeed, these sufferings were not in vain. Fox and his followers went to jail for their opinions, so that for some years three or four thousand of these conscientious people were in confinement, until it became plain that conscience was a power which could not be compelled. The Quakers, both in England and in New England, were contending for religious liberty. They went to prison until the laws which imprisoned honest people for their religious opinions were changed for very shame. In Massachusetts, where the Puritan law banished Quakers and declared that they would be hanged if they came back, four Quakers returned deliberately to be hanged, and were so put to death on Boston Common, in order to put an end to the law by showing, in the fact of their martyrdom, what an unrighteous law it was.

Fox was probably the most self-confident man in England; the most self-conceited, his enemies said. He was regarded by many wise and devout persons as a pestilent fellow. He was not only sure that he was right, but he was equally sure that most of his neighbors, even in the ministry, were wrong. He did not hesitate to assail Oliver Cromwell with exhortations to repent of his sins. But the patience with which many good people took his hard words shows that there was something fine and noble in the man. He was, no doubt, a disquieting person, whose speech was frank and stern, but so were all the ancient prophets. And the religion of his time needed his rebukes. It consisted too much in pious words and pious ways, without the reality of the spirit.

"He was a heavenly-minded man," said Thomas Ellwood, the friend of Milton, who edited George Fox's "Journal." "He was valiant for the truth, bold in asserting it, patient in suffering for it, unwearied in laboring in it, steady in his testimony to it, unmovable as a rock."

"The inwardness and weight of his spirit," said William Penn, his most distinguished disciple, "the reverence and solemnity of his address and behavior, and the fewness and fullness of his words, have often struck even strangers with admiration, as they used to reach others with consolation. The most awful living, reverent frame I ever felt or beheld, I must say, was his in prayer. In all things he acquitted himself like a man, yea, a strong man, a new and heavenly-minded man, and all of God Almighty's making." WESLEY
1703-1791

JOHN Wesley had fourteen brothers and sisters. One time, after he had become a man, he asked his mother to write out some of the methods which she had used in bringing up her large family, and her reply he copied in his journal. She taught her children, when they were punished, to cry softly, "by which means they escaped abundance of correction they might otherwise have had. " They were so constantly accustomed to eat and drink what was set before them, whether they liked it or not, that there was no difficulty in making them take medicine: "they durst not refuse it." Mrs. Wesley said that " in order to form the minds of children, the first thing to be done is to conquer their will, and bring them to an 396 JOHN WESLEY

From the Painting: by N. Hone in the National Portrait Gallery obedient temper." As soon as they could speak, they were taught the Lord's Prayer, which they said at rising and at bedtime, and " they were very early made to distinguish the Sabbath from other days." Every act of obedience, "especially when it crossed upon their own inclinations," was commended and rewarded. All property rights were very carefully observed. No child was "suffered to invade the property of another in the smallest matter, though it were but of the value of a farthing, or a pin." Every day the older children read aloud to the younger the Psalms for the day, out of the prayer-book, and a chapter of the Old Testament in the morning, and of the New Testament in the evening.

In this orderly household Wesley passed his early years. His father was a clergyman of the Church of England, and he was to follow in his steps. The life was strict and sober, but the children enjoyed themselves so much the more. They were very merry. It is remembered of John that he was "gay and sprightly, with a turn for wit and humor."

In due time he went to college at Oxford, and entered the ministry at the age of twenty-two. Part of his time he spent as an assistant in his father's parish, where he " read plays, attended the village fairs, shot plovers in the fenlands, and enjoyed a dance with his sisters," and perhaps with some who were not his sisters; besides attending to his more serious duties. But his chief interest was in the university. He was made a teacher of Greek there, and had a group of students about him whom he tutored.

All this time, religion was as natural to Wesley as eating and drinking. He was in no way disturbed by it, nor was he very earnestly concerned about it. His conscience did not trouble him. He was determined, however, to make the most of himself. He kept a diary in which he set down how he used his time; having his hours and tasks very carefully arranged,— this he would do at eight, and that at nine, and so on through the day. He began to read books of devotion, especially the writings of Thomas a Kempis. He gradually gathered about him a little company of Oxford men who agreed to spend their evenings together. On weekdays they read the classics aloud, and on Sundays the Greek Testament. More and more, the life of religion seemed to these young men to be the supreme thing. They made rules for themselves, fasting on Wednesdays and Fridays, and going to the Holy Communion every Sunday. One day they heard about a man who was in the Oxford jail for killing his wife, and they went to visit him. That led to other visits to the prisoners. Presently, they began to go about among the poor, praying with them and reading the Bible.

This behavior attracted attention in the university. And, curiously enough, very few liked it. The young tutors and fellows were laughed at. Their little association was called the Godly Club, or the Holy Club. The men were called Methodists, because they kept the rules of the Church, and tried to live the life of religion methodically. When they went to church, they found a crowd of students by the door waiting to jeer at them as they went in.

It is hard for us to-day to imagine a time when young men were made unpleasantly conspicuous by going to church. There are men, indeed, who do not go to church themselves, and are not interested in religion, but they commonly respect those who are. At Oxford, in the beginning of the eighteenth century, men who showed an uncommon interest in religion were not respected. They were called hypocrites.

This was largely on account of a general dislike of Puritans. The great Puritan movement had been followed by reaction. The English people were like young men who have been brought up so strictly that when they get their own way at last they rebel against everything which they have been taught. Having been compelled to go to church, they resolve that they will never go again, and they devote themselves to the pleasures which were forbidden them at home. When the Puritan Commonwealth was over, and the monarchy and the Church were restored, a great part of the nation rejoiced in a new liberty. "Now," they said, "we will have a good time." They hated the very name of Puritan. It meant a long face, and a constant habit of quoting from the Bible, and a disapproval of even innocent amusement. It was represented by the Puritan minister at a wedding who congratulated himself that his presence there had banished all carnal joy from the occasion. The result was that all earnestness in religion was associated by many people with the days which they remembered with dislike. John Wesley and his Methodists at Oxford were suspected of being Puritans.

Wesley's enthusiasm led him to become a missionary. At that time, any zealous person who wished to do difficult mission work came to America. Thus Wesley took ship for Georgia, intending to devote himself to the conversion of the American Indians.

Among his companions on the sea were certain German emigrants who were of the Moravian religion. The early Moravians were disciples of John Hus. After many persecutions they had fled from Moravia, and a company of them had been invited by Count Zinzendorf to settle on his estates in Saxony. There they had built a town called Herrnhut. They had become a society in the Lutheran

Church, as the Franciscans and the Jesuits were societies in the Roman Church. Out of Herrnhut these German emigrants had come, offering themselves for Christian work in Georgia. Now, on the voyage, there was a tremendous storm, and the wind split the mainsail, and the ship seemed likely to go down. But while most of the passengers were greatly excited and overcome with terror, the Moravians said their prayers with entire serenity of spirit and seemed quite ready to accept, with cheerfulness, whatever came, whether life or death. Wesley felt that they had something in their religion which he lacked.

They all arrived in Georgia safely, and Wesley was put in charge of the parish of Savannah. But the Indians were in the woods, and Wesley could not reach them. Even the English did not receive him with much satisfaction, for immediately he insisted on applying to the people there in the wilderness the rules which he and the Holy Club had kept at Oxford. He proposed to have all the provisions of the prayer-book observed strictly. He declared that infants must be baptized by immersion, because that method was given the preference in the book. He required that everybody who intended to come to the Holy Communion must give notice the day before, according to the book. And one young woman who had neglected to give such notice he repelled from the Lord's Table. Unhappily, this young woman had been so great a friend of Wesley's that he had asked her to marry him, and she had declined, and had married another. The young minister's action was laid to jealousy and anger. And all her friends were so indignant about it that Wesley thought it wise to bring his ministry in Savannah to a rather abrupt close. He suddenly departed from the town, and from the colony, and returned to England.

One of the complaints against Wesley was that he introduced new hymns into the service of the Church. He published, in Charleston, in 1737, a book of Psalms and Hymns, some of which he had translated from the German. It was the beginning of a new use of music in the eighteenth century for the stirring of religious emotion. The singing at revival meetings goes back for its origin to Wesley's book. The hymns of Charles Wesley contributed almost as much to the renewal of religion in England as the sermons of John.

Also, in Savannah, Wesley formed a society. He had in his congregation a company of devout persons who met together like the Holy Club at Oxford. They began and ended their meetings with singing and praying, and in the midst of these exercises they read the Bible and talked about it. It was the idea which was at the heart of the administration of the great movement which Wesley was soon to start—this assembly of like-minded persons to pray and sing and speak together directly and informally.

Wesley said, the year before he died, "I do not remember to have felt lowness of spirits for a quarter of an hour since I was born." His journal shows, however, that he returned from Georgia much depressed. He felt that he had made a failure of his ministry. On the return voyage there was another dangerous storm, and he remembered the Moravians. He doubted if he had ever in his life been a good Christian. He perceived that all his excellent doctrines, and his endeavors to grow in grace by means of the customs and sacraments of the Church, still left him cold. He seemed to himself like a house well-built, but neither warmed nor lighted. Looking back over his ministry in later life, he said that thus far his labors bore no fruit, because at first he "took for granted that all his hearers were believers and that many of them needed no repentance."

Arrived in London, Wesley found a young Moravian named Peter Bohler. Bohler told him that what he needed was faith: not faith in the sense of accepting certain articles of belief, but faith as Luther taught it, meaning a real and personal approach to Christ. And Bohler said that this living faith comes definitely, often suddenly, into the soul. Bohler told Wesley that what he needed was to be converted, and by conversion he meant this sudden emotion, this feeling of assurance of salvation.

On the twenty-fourth of May, 1738, Wesley opened his Bible early in the morning, and looked to see what text would meet his eye, and it was St. Paul's saying about "great and precious promises." In the afternoon, he attended the service at St. Paul's Cathedral, and was deeply impressed by the anthem, which was the psalm called De Profundis— "Out of the deep have I called unto thee, O Lord." In the evening he went to a little devotional meeting where the speaker was discussing Luther's Preface to the Epistle to the Romans. "About a quarter before nine," says Wesley, "while he was describing the change which God works in the heart through faith in Christ, I felt my heart strangely moved. I felt I did trust in Christ, Christ alone, for salvation, and an assurance was given me that He had taken away *my* sins, even *mine,* and saved *me* from the law of sin and death."

This experience was the beginning of a new kind of ministry. Wesley began to bring others into his own religious happiness. At first in Fetter Lane, then in a foundry in Moorfields, he preached his new gospel, and began the formation of a new society. He may have remembered how Francis founded the Franciscans and Dominic the Dominicans; he may have had in mind the society of the Moravians, within the Lutheran Church; or he may have been conscious only of the human impulses which call people together into organization. Whatever the reason, Wesley set about the establishment of societies. He was not content with appealing to the people, and bringing them into a new way of living, he made the appeal effective and kept them in the new way by organizing them into bands. He had a genius for that kind of work. Wherever he went he found a great response of emotion, people groaned and cried, sometimes they fainted; Wesley hardly knew whether it was the work of good spirits or bad. But he never failed to see to it that the people thus affected and converted were put under instruction and oversight. There were necessary expenses connected with the meetings, and the people were asked to pay a penny a week. One man said, "I will pay my penny and collect the money of eleven others." Wesley made these twelve into a "class," and the collector was the "leader." When they brought their pennies, they stayed for prayers; they talked together concerning their various religious experiences, speaking of their temptations and trials and of the divine assistance. By-and-by, to experience meetings were added conferences, and watchnights, and love-feasts. In order to enter the society one must have a desire to flee from wrath to come and to be saved from sin; and evidences of salvation must be shown " by doing no harm, by doing good of every possible sort, by attending on all the means of grace." The societies bore the name by which Wesley had been called at Oxford; they were called Methodists. And all the Methodists belonged to the Church of England, as all the Franciscans belonged to the Church of Rome. The new preaching attracted crowds of hearers. Partly because it was new, but much more because it was plain and earnest and direct, people came to hear it. Many who listened felt that the preacher spoke straight to their own souls. They felt the burden of their sins, and he told them how to get rid of it by giving themselves to Jesus Christ. "Victory over sin was the goal which he set before all his people." He went about, as his Master had gone, among the poorest people. He found them ignorant, indifferent to religion, and drunken. It seemed to him that nobody was caring for their souls.

At first he preached in pulpits, but many of the regular ministers did not like what he said. And whether they liked it or not, the congregations were too big for the churches. He began to preach in the churchyards, and in the streets, and in the open fields. People came in thousands. Thus he went from one town to another. Early in his ministry he formed the habit of getting up every morning at four o'clock; and almost every day he preached at five. For years he traveled five thousand miles a year and preached fifteen sermons every week.

He had to have assistance, but he could not find ministers enough to help him. Some did not approve of him, some could not leave their parishes. He made preachers out of the people. Presently he had a hundred earnest men who had been converted by his preaching, and were going out to preach to others. The movement extended out of England into Ireland, into Scotland, into America. It aroused the whole English-speaking people.

Wesley met with continual opposition. People hooted at him, and stoned him. Sometimes when he spoke in a churchyard, they rang the bells so that his voice could not be heard. In one place they drove a herd of cows in among the congregation as they stood in the street. In another place, "we came into the town," says Wesley, "about eleven; and many people seemed very desirous to hear for themselves, concerning the way which is everywhere spoken against; but it could not be; the sons of Belial gathered themselves together, headed by one or two wretches called gentlemen; and continued shouting, cursing, blaspheming, and throwing showers of stones, almost without intermission. So that after some time spent in prayer for them, I judged it best to dismiss the congregation."

One time a mob beset the house where he was staying. "Bring out the minister!" they cried, "we will have the minister!" Wesley went out and "spoke a few words, which God applied," and they all cried with might and main, "The gentleman is an honest gentleman, and we will spill our blood in his defense." One day he writes in his journal, "To attempt speaking was vain, for the noise on every side was like the roaring of the sea; so they dragged me along till we came to the town, where seeing the door of a large house open I attempted to go in; but a man, catching me by the hair, pulled me back into the middle of the mob. I broke out aloud into prayer. And now the man who had just before headed the mob, turned and said, 'Sir, I will spend my life for you; follow me and not one soul here shall touch a hair of your head.'" And Wesley adds, "from the beginning to the end I found the same presence of mind as if I had been sitting in my own study."

Thus he preached day after day. His journal reads like the account in the Acts of the missionary journeys of St. Paul.

But there were attentive congregations, too. "In the midst of the sermon, a large cat, frighted out of a chamber, leaped down upon a woman's head, and ran over the heads and shoulders of many more; but none of them moved, or cried out, any more than if it had been a butterfly."

Wherever he went, the sick were made well by his prayers. "I dined with one," he says, "who told me in all simplicity, 'Sir, I thought last week that there could be no such rest as you described; none in this world, wherein we could be so free, as not to desire ease in pain; but God has taught me better; for on Friday and Saturday, when I was in the strongest pain, I never once had a moment's desire of ease, but only that the will of God might be done.'" And in many places the results were such as were described among the miners of Kingswood. "Kingswood does not now, as it did a year ago, resound with cursing and blasphemy. It is no more filled with drunkenness and uncleanness, and the idle diversions that naturally lead thereto. It is no longer full of wars and fightings, of clamor and bitterness, of wrath and envyings: peace and love are there."

Wesley ministered not only to the souls but to the minds of the poor people. "No man in the eighteenth century did so much to create a taste for good reading, and to supply them with books at the lowest prices." This printing became a great business, and the money which Wesley made by it he used for the relief of poverty. He provided those who were in distress with clothes and food. He established lending offices for the help of struggling business men. To all these interests he brought his wonderful genius for organization. He changed the life of England.

All this time, the Methodists were a society in the English Church. Wesley would not allow them to hold their meetings at the hours when there was service in the parish churches. They were sent to the regular ministers for the sacraments. But in America the Church of England had no bishops. There was great need of supervision and nobody to supervise. And at last Wesley appointed men for the American work, who were at first called superintendents, but were soon called bishops. Wesley felt, indeed, that he was himself a bishop by the grace of God, as St. Paul was. But the final result was separation. During Wesley's life the Methodist societies continued in the Church, but when the end of his long labors came, the desire of the leading Methodists waited no longer. Out they came into independence.

Wesley lived through the hard days of opposition into a time when almost all men revered him. He was recognized in England as one who belonged with the saints and the apostles. One who knew him in those days said, "So fine an old man I never saw. The happiness of his mind beamed forth in his countenance." He might well be happy. He had served God with all his strength; he had saved souls; he had fought the good fight; he knew that there was laid up for him the crown of righteousness which is the reward of the faithful servants of God.

LIFE-STORIES FOR THE YOUNG *Dean Hodges'* SAINTS AND HEROES: To the End of the Middle Ages.
Illustrated. $1.35 net.

Biographies of Cyprian, Athanasius, Ambrose, Chrysostom, Jerome, Augustine, Benedict, Gregory the Great, Columba, Charlemagne, Hildebrand, Anselm, Bernard, Becket, Langton, Dominic, Francis, Wycliffe, Hus, Savonarola.

Each of these men was a great person in his time, and represented its best qualities. Their dramatic and adventurous experiences make the story of their lives interesting as well as inspiring and suggestive.

Church history and doctrine are touched upon only as they develop in the biographies.

"Here is much important history told in a readable and attractive manner, and from the standpoint which makes history most vivid and most likely to remain fixed in memory, namely, the standpoint of the individual actor."—*Springfield Republican.* *Dean Hodges'* SAINTS AND HEROES: Since the Middle Ages
Illustrated. $1.35 net.

The new volume includes biographies of Luther, More, Loyola, Cranmer, Calvin, Knox, Coligny, William the Silent, Laud, Cromwell, Fox, Wesley, Bunyan and Brewster.

John Buchan's SIR WALTER RALEIGH
With double-page pictures in color; cover linings. Square l2mo. Price, $2.00 net.

A life of Raleigh told in eleven chapters. Each chapter covers some important scene in his life and is told by some friend or follower as if seen with his own eyes. Some of the characters are invented, but all that they tell really happened.

The narrative has spirit, color, and atmosphere, and is unusually well written.

America figures largely in the story, and American boys will enjoy this book.

HENRY HOLT AND COMPANY PUBLISHERS Viii'12 NEW YORK *For Young Folks from 9 to 16 Years old.* PARTNERS FOR FAIR
With illustrations by Faith Avery. $1.25 net.

A story full of action, not untinged by pathos, of a boy and his faithful dog and their wanderings after the poorhouse burns down. They have interesting experiences with a traveling circus; the boy is thrown from a moving train, and has a lively time with the Mexican Insurrectos, from whom he is rescued by our troops.

THE LUCK OF THE DUDLEY GRAHAMS
Illustrated by Francis Day. 300 pp., i2mo. $1.50. A family story of city life. Lightened by humor and an airship.

"Among the very best of books for young folks. Appeals especially to girls."—*Wisconsin List for Township Libraries.*

"Promises to be perennially popular. A family of happy, healthy, inventive, bright children make the best of restricted conditions and prove themselves masters of circumstances."—*Christian Register.*

"Sparkles with cleverness and humor."—*Brooklyn Eagle.* COCK-A-DOODLE HILL

A sequel to the above. Illustrated by Francis Day. 296 pp., i2mo. $1.50. "Cockle-a-doodle Hill" is where the Dudley Graham family went to live when they left New York, and here Ernie started her chicken-farm, with one solitary fowl, "Hennerietta." The pictures of country scenes and the adventures and experiences of this household of young people are very life-like.

"No better book for young people than 'The Luck of the Dudley Grahams' was offered last year. 'Cock-a-Doodle Hill' is another of similar qualities."—*Philadelphia Press.* HENRY HOLT AND COMPANY PUBLISHERS (vm'12) NEW YORK

CPSIA information can be obtained
at www.ICGtesting.com
Printed in the USA
LVOW05s0342180817
545480LV00014B/565/P